Light in the Midst of Zion

A History of Black Baptists in Utah

1892-1996

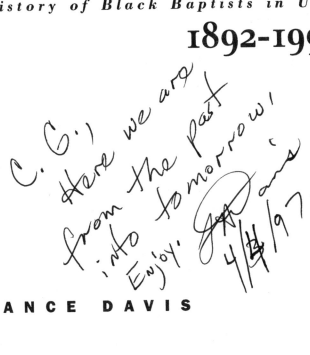

C. G.,
Here we are
from the past
into tomorrow!
Enjoy! *[signature]* Davis
4/4/97

by
FRANCE DAVIS

printed in the United States of America
production by Idrees Khan
cover photo by Brett Colvin
cover design by Joseph Briggs

ISBN 0-9656532-1-8

TM
UNIVERSITY PUBLISHING,LLC
P.O. Box 520755, Salt Lake City, Utah 84152
801-521-7090

Contents

Forward

Light in the Midst of Zion by France A. Davis, is a history of Salt Lake City's Calvary Missionary Baptist Church and the Black baptist churches in Utah over the past 100 plus years. The result of painstaking research and several interviews, the study is an important account of the efforts of Black Utah baptists to establish churches of their own in a state where 70 percent of the population are members of the Church of Jesus Christ of Latter-Day Saints (LDS) and where African Americans constitute less than one percent of the state's population.

The primary reason Calvary Missionary Baptist Church and the other Black baptist congregations were formed was to address the spiritual needs of African American baptists in Utah. Calvary is the largest predominantly Black congregation in Utah. Along with meeting the spiritual needs of its membership, Calvary and its sister churches play a major role in serving the secular needs of the African American community in the state.

Reverend Davis provides a wonderful journey into the past of a small western Black community struggling to develop and sustain churches where they could exercise autonomy in their decisions and provide their members with a spiritual, social, and cultural connection to the larger, national, Black community. The sense of connection with the larger African American community has been critical to Black Utahns in their efforts to sustain themselves in a place where their numbers are few and where they have faced racism and discrimination similar to their brothers and sisters in other parts of the United States. Davis tells about some of the schisms that developed in a few congregations and how the members responded to their respective situations.

The biographical sketches of Black religious leaders and lay men and women who played important roles in their churches

1

are striking. In addition to working on church matters, several of these individuals were active leaders in non-church activities in the field of civil rights. The work of Reverend George Hart(s) in organizing a local branch of the National Association for the Advancement of Colored People is an example of the dual role of a Black minister. The late Mrs. Mignon Richmond, who has a city park named in her honor, served in leadership positions in Calvary Missionary Baptist Church and found time to work as a community organizer, helping to improve opportunities for people of color residing in the central city section of Salt Lake City.

Anyone seeking to learn about the history of Blacks in Utah and how they forged a sense of community among themselves must read *Light in the Midst of Zion*. Reverend Davis' book illustrates how African American baptists who settled in Utah transported their religious institutions to the land of Zion and reestablished their spiritual roots in a new land. For Black Utahns, the African American church has historically been the single most important institution in the state. It has served as a place of refuge in the most difficult times and many of the Black religious leaders have been ambassadors of good will for the African American, and larger, community.

Ronald G. Coleman, Ph.D.
University of Utah

Preface

As I travel across the country, I inevitably hear the following inquiry: "You say you are from Utah? You must be the only Black living there!" Those I meet, particularly but not exclusively African Americans, find it strange that I am a resident of the Salt Lake City, Utah community. Their image of this community does not lend itself to one in which African Americans are communal participants, especially when they happen to be Baptist as well- non members of Salt Lake City's dominant religious culture, The Church of Jesus Christ of Latter-day Saints (LDS), the Mormons.

On one occasion, I attended a meeting in Denver, Colorado to discuss procedures for receiving federal funds already allocated. The Calvary Missionary Baptist Church of Salt Lake City, Utah had managed to gain full community support and be awarded a federal government loan to build a housing complex for the elderly. The regional director of Housing and Urban Development entered the room and promptly announced, "I just want to see that African-American man who is a Baptist living in Utah with letters of support from all the politicians." Then, he called me by my name and asked me to stand.

By this time, I had served as pastor of the Calvary Missionary Baptist Church for fifteen years, and was seeking funds to build a senior citizen home adjacent to the church, in order to have the church meet the needs of an important segment of our community, as well as to continue a well-established tradition of providing service and playing more than a spiritual role in this community. This experience, among many that could be offered, underscores the need to make available historic information about the African American presence in Utah, in general, and particularly about Utah's Black Baptist Churches, and specifically the pioneering congregation of Calvary Missionary Baptist Church in Salt Lake City.

Among all the histories of African American experiences, that of the role of the church speaks most about our heritage. *The Bible* puts it best, "The boundary lines have fallen for me in pleasant places; I have a goodly heritage." (Psalm 16:6 NRSV) Only to the degree that we know and rehearse where we have come from do we appreciate and celebrate the past. Thus, this book project grew out of my perceived need to document the history of African Americans and their experiences in Utah, and specifically to note their successful effort to carve out for themselves a place to worship through the denomination(s) of their choice.

Limitations of This Study

This researcher has searched long and hard for information to make this study meaningful and complete. Through various sources, much has been discovered that was not previously documented. Yet, many questions cannot be answered from the limited traditional sources. For Church records are, at best, sparse. Very limited correspondence remains available perhaps due to two primary reasons. First, Black Baptists tend to communicate more orally than in writing. The oral tradition does not lend itself readily to documentation. Second, with pastor turn over being so high, personal papers were either discarded or taken away when pastors moved to another work.

Further, this study is limited because very little biographical information is available about former pastors and church members. Who they were, where they came from, their training and formal education, and the reasons for their coming and going were seldom recorded in early records.

A third limitation of this study comes from the minimal coverage of Black Baptists by local newspapers. On the one hand, Blacks newspapers like *the Broad Ax*, *The Western Light*, and *the*

Utah Plain Dealer, did not continue publishing for the long term. Their coverage was more thorough but not for long periods of time. A fourth such paper, *Tri-City Oracle*, published weekly by Reverend James W. Washington appears to have survived only during 1902. On the other hand, the three major White dailies of Salt Lake City and Ogden failed to give much attention to news in the Black community except for superstars and criminals.

Thus, any "missing" information in this study of Black Baptists in Utah is due to the availability of source materials and not to omissions on the part of the researcher. That may also be one of the reasons why no one has completed a more adequate study earlier.

Research Methodology

Traditional research sources such as correspondence, diaries histories, church files, etc. have been very limited in this study of Black Baptists in Utah. However, themes have emerged and are fleshed out by oral interviews. From memory and private collections, long term residents shared their experiences and insights. These personal histories contribute to understanding as well as share feelings about the experiences. Thus, I am indebted to the pastors and members who told their stories with great passion to be used in this work.

Historical Significance

This work fills a major void in the recording of the history of Blacks in Utah and the United States of America. While earlier works by such historians as Ronald G. Coleman, Helen Z. Papanikolas, Larry Gerlach, and Leslie Kelen explore generally the history of Blacks in Utah, the role of the Churches has not yet received due attention.

Further, the numerous studies of the LDS Church as well as those studies of the Catholic, Episcopal, Presbyterian, and indeed

American and Southern Baptists in Utah illustrate the importance of understanding the spiritual as well as the secular experiences of Utah's people. With the Churches playing such a significant role in the lives of Blacks, the important history of Black Baptists in Utah cannot be ignored.

Finally, not much has been written about Blacks Churches in the intermountain and western states. While Dr. Mamie Oliver wrote a history of St. Paul Baptist Church of Boise, Idaho and Mary Watkins recently completed a project about the Bethel Baptist Church of Pocatello, Idaho, this book is a pioneering effort about Black Baptists in Utah.

Thus, this book will include collected facts and personal stories with memories. It will set a pattern and make a lasting contribution toward the understanding of the Black religious experience in Utah, the west, and the United States.

Chapter 1: "In the Beginning They Were One" delineates the history of the Black Baptist Church in Utah. It demonstrates that with the founding of the Calvary Missionary Baptist Church congregation the Black Baptist church preceded the statehood of Utah. She is the "Mother Church" of Black Baptists in Utah.

Chapter 2: "Scattering Brotherhood" provides an overview of the emergence of several African American religious congregations in Utah, in addition to the Calvary Missionary Baptist Church, and discusses the founding of the Association of Baptist Churches (ABC). This chapter also records the organization and support of additional para-church bodies.

Chapter 3: "They Who Overcome" focuses on the growth and survival of Baptist congregations during various historical junctures of difficulty and hardships, including the Great Depression and World War II.

Chapter 4: "Spreading The Light" discusses the work of several congregations and the related bodies. It highlights the various roles of the Black Baptist churches throughout Utah. The interrelatedness of these congregations is the central focus.

Chapter 5: "Light That Cannot Be Hidden" deals with the unwavering determination of Black Baptists to carry on in Utah. It looks at the work done through organizations larger and outside of the local congregation. Recent works in missions at home and abroad along with regional educational efforts are included.

Chapter 6: "Epilogue" looks at the overall high-watermarks of the Black Baptist Church in Utah. In addition to viewing and commenting on some of its weaknesses and strengths, this chapter includes future projections for the existing congregations.

Acknowledgements

I give special thanks to my wife Willene Davis for her patience and understanding. Also, thanks to Sylvia Morris, Tauni Lee, Mrs. Gladys Hesleph, Brenda Tanner, Shauna Robertson, Mrs. Doris Frye and the entire Calvary Missionary Baptist Church congregation for their support and help in the writing of this book. This book is dedicated to my wife and family, and the Calvary Missionary Baptist congregation as well as the pastors and congregations of Black Baptist congregations in Utah.

I offer further thanks to all the pastors, congregations and individuals who shared both written and verbal information. Your kindness will always be cherished and appreciated. Thank you for keeping records and photographs down through the years.

Special thanks to Richard W. Shorthill for his long hours of work to insure clear photographs, maps, and art work.

The suggestions of my colleagues Dr. Larry R. Gerlach, Dr. Wilfred Samuels, Dr. Ronald G. Coleman, and Dr. Mark McPhail have been invaluable in the structure and completeness of this project.

Introduction

Would you believe a Black Baptist Church existed in Utah before Utah became a state? Would you believe a church fund raiser with more "'Possum" than you have ever seen and with all the "pickaninnies" playing around? Would you believe an African-American church where those with dark skin sat on one side and those with light skin sat on the other? Would you believe a church building whose floor was so weak that a funeral home director refused to place a casket on it? Would you believe it is possible to collect enough dimes to build a new, modern church building?

Well, believe it! These facts are all true. They are central to the composite history of the Calvary Missionary Baptist Church, the first Black Baptist church in Salt Lake City, Utah. Which is not to mention the similar challenges and experiences of other Black Baptists. Here is how it happened.

As early as 1824, the son of a Missouri planter and a slave woman traveled and worked in what was then the territory of Utah. It was still part of Mexico at that time. James P. Beckworth, a frontier mountain man, was a blacksmith with the Ashley Fur Trapping Expedition. The group hunted, fished, and trapped in the Uinta and Rocky Mountains. To store their furs, caches were dug and part of the valley became known as "Cache Valley." Beckworth, an African-American, discovered and laid out the pass through the Sierra Nevada mountains between Reno and the California line that bears his name.[1]

Among the early settlers moving into the Salt Lake valley in 1847, the year specifically associated with the arrival of the first Mormon settlers led by their prophet, Brigham Young, were at least three African-Americans: Oscar Crosby, Green Flake and Hark Lay. Their names are listed on various historic documents and inscribed on the "This Is The Place" and the "Brigham

Young" monuments. They were slaves or servants sent to prepare a place in the Salt Lake valley by their Mississippi masters. Additional African-Americans came to the Utah territory during subsequent years. In 1853, Elijah Abel, who had been previously ordained to the Melchizedek priesthood (the highest level to which most Mormon males are ordained), served as a carpenter helping to build the Salt Lake City Temple of the Church of Jesus Christ of Latter-day Saints. He and his wife Mary Ann simultaneously operated the Farnham Hotel.

By 1860, there were 59 Blacks, approximately 30 of whom were slaves ofttimes called "colored servants," living in Utah according to the Bureau of Census. Freedom came when President Abraham Lincoln signed the Emancipation Proclamation, in 1863, during the Civil War. Slavery was officially abolished when Congress amended the United States Constitution through the Thirteenth Amendment. Blacks such as Elijah Abel and Green Flake were listed as heads of households in the 1870 and 1880 census records. Thirty years later, according to the census records of 1890, there were as many as 500 blacks in the Utah territory.[2]

The number of African-Americans in this territory remained small until three major economic changes occurred during the later half of the 1800s. First, the railroad industry, centered in the Ogden and Price/Helper areas, coupled with mining, employed Black men on their work crews. This railroad hub between 1870 and 1910 included the Union Pacific, Central Pacific, Denver and Rio Grande, Oregon Short Line and Los Angeles-Salt Lake Railway. Second, several hotels and saloons recruited and hired southern Blacks to perform menial tasks, including chamber maids, porters, waiters, cooks, redcaps, and parlor attendants. Similar duties were performed by Blacks in the private home of wealthy Utah residents. Third, the United States Army stationed Black troops of the 10th Cavalry and the 24th Infantry at Fort Douglas and Fort Duchesne, which doubled the population of Utah Blacks between 1896 and

1899. (Noting their coarse, nappy hair, while recognizing the bravery of these Black soldiers, the Indians called them "Buffalo Soldiers.") In addition, these more stationery African-American populations were impacted as well by the westward frontier movement. "There were many people who stopped off in Salt Lake City who were on their way to the California Gold Rush, hoping they might strike it rich in a gold mine. Some never got any further west than Salt Lake."[3]

A few Black owned businesses began to emerge during the later half of the 1800s. They included a restaurant at 153 South Main Street owned and operated by Frances H. Grice. The conflict which resulted in the lynching of Sam Joe Harvey on August 25, 1883 in downtown Salt Lake City started at this place of business.[4] In addition, Frances H. Grice, John Burns, Allen Smith, Andrew Campbell, and A. D. McAlfred organized the Elevator Prospecting Company, a black mining company.[5]

At least two Black owned newspapers were published in Salt Lake City during the last decade of 1800. *The Broad Ax* was launched in 1895 with Julius F. Taylor as editor and the Utah *Plain Dealer* followed in 1897 with William W. Taylor as editor. Both papers continued into the early 1900s. Interestingly, *The Broad Ax* was revived in 1973 for a short time.

The First African-American Institution in Utah

The exclusivity practiced by the dominant local religious community, coupled with the overt and covert practices of segregation in the United States at the turn of the century, mandated that Utah's African Americans consciously eke out a place for themselves in Zion. Finding themselves in only limited roles or completely excluded from the public institutions of the greater Salt Lake City community, the growing Black population organized its own institutions, religious, educational, political.

In 1890, the Trinity African Methodist Episcopal Church (AME) came into being as the earliest Black religious institution on record in Salt Lake City, Utah. Reverend T. Saunders organized the congregation which held her initial meetings in member homes and rented facilities. In the early years, this congregation became one of two primary gathering place for African-American youth. The Trinity African Methodist Episcopal congregation continues to survive and operate in her historic structure, built in 1902, at 239 East 600 South, renamed Martin Luther King, Jr. Boulevard. She stands as a testimony to the strength and determination of African-American Methodist in Utah.

During the same general time period, Black Baptists in Utah felt the need to have their spiritual needs met as well. They wanted to take the spiritual fires burning on the inside and show them through a visible institution. Shortly thereafter, the Calvary Missionary Baptist Church of Salt Lake City would be established. This congregation became the second primary gathering place for African-American youth activities, and would emerge as not only the largest, but also as the most influential and well-known of Utah's Black churches. She would go on to be seen as the cradle and foundation of other Black Baptist Churches in Utah from Mohrland to Ogden.

The record will show that the humble and largely unnoticed beginnings of Calvary Missionary Baptist Church belie her enduring strength and longevity. Little notice has been given to the fact that many of the other Black Baptist congregations and para-church organizations in Utah can trace their roots directly to Calvary. In fact, this account offers a historical perspective demonstrating the links between Calvary Missionary Baptist Church and a number of other predominately African-American institutions.

Chapter 1
In the Beginning They Were One

Black Baptists who moved into Utah primarily for better work opportunity, sought to make the experience positive spiritually. They wanted their new homeland to be indeed their new home to nurture their spiritual fervor and fellowship.

Calvary Missionary Baptist Church

About twelve years after Reverend William W. Cooley summoned approximately 150 Black Baptist leaders on November 24-26, 1880 to Montgomery, Alabama for the noble purpose of organizing a National Baptist Convention,[6] the Calvary Missionary Baptist Church originated in Salt Lake City, Utah. Fully four years before the territory would become a state, in 1892, this congregation became the first organized group of Black Baptists gathered for worship in Utah.

In 1892, a small group of Black women came together to pray. Meeting in various private homes, they were soon designated the "Baptist Prayer Band." They assembled under the leadership of Sister Emma Jackson, the widow of George Jackson who had lived at 176 East 700 South, and her home became their primary meeting place.[7] Most likely "Mom Jack," as she was affectionately known, initially called the group together regularly for worship, to pray to God, and to read God's Word from The Bible. "Mom Jack" continued to serve among the congregational leadership until the mid-nineteen twenties. These strong, Black women worked long hours in private homes including that of the Governor as maids, cooks, and wash ladies. At the same time, they kept their own houses, tended their children, and cared for their husbands. They turned to Black centers of worship, havens of fellowship, which provide positive image, personal strength and responsible participation in community building.

Early Baptisms

On the Sunday prior to April 18, 1896, the "Baptist Prayer Band" met with and used the facilities of the First Baptist Church at the corner of Second South and Second West. The building was filled with people and the Reverend George Maney, First Baptist's pastor, preached a powerful sermon from Matthew 19:28. After singing hymns 150 and 120 and being led in prayer by Brother Williams W. Taylor, the pastor performed the "colored baptizing." Mrs. Emma Hatfield, Mrs. Mattie Ketchell, and Mrs. Eliza McAfee were the three earliest candidates baptized into the Calvary Missionary Baptist Church on that Sunday.[8]

Many of the early participants, having come from the southern states, brought with them their spiritual fervor, the beat of the drum, and the burning desire to worship and praise God. The emotionally charged participatory worship form drew others as they moved across the community. Unlike the worship atmosphere in many other worship experiences, African-Americans worshipped with energetic vigor and spiritual fervor. Black baptists soon outgrew the space available in private homes. They needed and wanted a place set aside and dedicated solely to Christian worship. For some reason, the group experienced a dry spell and reached out for help. The Reverend Richard Quarles assisted the congregation during that period of idleness and inactivity starting the fall of 1896.

First Officials and Building

Some weeks prior to June 15, 1898, a few of the faithful members of the Calvary Missionary Baptist Church invited the Reverend A. E. Reynolds to permanently start the work. On June 18, 1898, he announced in the Black owned newspaper, *The Broad*

Ax, published by Julius F. Taylor in Salt Lake City, that a building was secured in the rear of the First Baptist Church at 315 West Second South. It appears the Calvary Missionary Baptist Church moved into that building and worshipped for a time. The earliest list of church officials identified the Reverend A. E. Reynolds as pastor, William S. Wearing and David Taylor as deacons, Oliver Stallworth as church clerk, and Louisa (Louise) Thompson, whom *The Broad Ax* described as "one of the brightest members of our race here in our city, as treasurer.[9] The public was invited to attend Sunday services at 10:30 A. M., Sunday School at 3:00 P. M., and prayer meeting every Thursday evening.[10]

After he arrived to guide the Calvary congregation, Reverend A. E. Reynolds called the people together at that location for Black Baptists to conduct worship in their own style and manner. However, according to the *Salt Lake Herald Newspaper*, the small band of believers soon found and moved into an old frame building located at 37 1/2 or 39 1/2 South West Temple Street.

This is the same space where Salt Lake City's Crossroad Mall parking structure stands in 1996. The newspaper described the church building as a "little colored house of worship in the alley off West Temple Street." The newly stabilized Calvary congregation worshiped freely in their new home, according to their own culture and desires. More important, this first congregation of Black Baptists committed themselves to teaching people how to do things the "Jesus way." Reverend Reynolds led the congregation for only about six months.

By January 28, 1899, the Reverend D. Jones from Topeka, Kansas had assumed the leadership of Calvary Missionary Baptist Church. Both church members and the community at large were encouraged to hear him preach that last Sunday night in January. He stirred the crowd and made a positive impression on those attending. Unfortunately, what started as a moving experience came to an abrupt end when Reverend Jones moved away the next year.

One of the ongoing problems confronting this new congregation was getting pastors to Utah and getting them to stay once they arrived. A number of major factors contributed to this problem. First, letter writing and word-of-mouth communications from Utah Blacks to Blacks in other areas of the country took time. Second, money was not easy to come by. In fact, offerings were ofttimes less than $1.00 per service. Third, the Black community did not have many residents and only a percentage of those attended and supported the churches. Fourth, the community offered pastors minimal opportunities for religious education and fellowship with other pastors. Thus, finding someone willing to come to Utah took months even years, and getting them to stay created further problems.

Celebration and Building

Perhaps the most exciting and energetic leader for the congregation in those early days came in 1901. Reverend James W. Washington brought his great leadership skills, a wealth of pastoral experience, and plans for building a sanctuary to Salt Lake City. His leadership and building experience included having served as a 2nd lieutenant of Company K, Eighth Illinois, the only regiment entirely directed by colored officers, during the War with Spain, and having raised and expended some $11,000.00 erecting the Rock Island McKinley Chapel. Reverend Washington "determined to see the congregation housed in a comfortable house...,a lot...purchased, and a stone edifice large enough to accommodate the congregation ...erected."[11] Reverend Washington declared emphatically that he would "not let anything go undone that will advance the cause of his people."[12]

Reverend Washington employed his creative skills and initiated two weeks of evangelistic outreach at the beginning of 1902. Gospel meetings were held every evening of the week. After the first week, he inspired and stirred the congregation with his sermon entitled "Never A Man Spake Like This Man," at the 8 p.m. Sunday worship services.[13] As the two weeks of Gospel meetings closed on February 2, 1902, "a special programme in honor of the late President William McKinley's birthday" was held at 3:30 p.m. The sermon topic for the 8 p.m. service which followed was "Prodigal Son." These sermons described the focus of worship while issuing a call for congregants to return home spiritually.

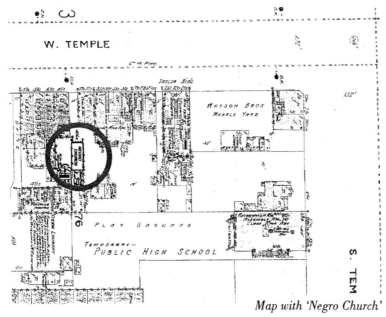

Map with 'Negro Church'

Building Fund 'Possum Festival

Under the leadership of Reverend Washington, the Calvary Missionary Baptist Church congregation outgrew its physical space, requiring the construction of a new building. That growth resulted from both the increasing Black population and the outreach of Reverend Washington and the congregation. As part of their building fund activities, the congregation hosted a 'possum dinner on February 8, 1902. *The Salt Lake Herald* describes the festivities as an "elaborate spread that threw the colored population into a state of joyous excitement." Meeting at 37 1/2 or 39½ South West Temple, the regular worship services included preaching at 11:15 a.m. and Sunday School at 12:30 p.m. That evening worship at 8 p.m. was led by Pastor James W. Washington preaching on the sermonic topic, "The Wagon That The World Used To Ride In." [14]

THE SALT LAKE TRIBUNE   Saturday, February 8, 1902

WAS REAL 'POSSUM DINNER

Elaborate Spread That Threw the Colored Population of Salt Lake Into a State of Joyous Excitement.

RAID ON THE 'POSSUM.

'Possum meat an' good an' sweet,
'Um-m-m-m! Oh, myrh!
'Possum meat on rough I'll eat,
Oh, lah', tha' I dida!

MALLORD BLANCHERS

The overall festivity was a tremendous successful communal affair, given Reverend Washington's overall objectives. A minister of "considerable note," Reverend Washington who had recently come to the area, planned "to erect a handsome church building within the near future." This genuine, old-fashioned 'possum dinner was the first effort toward raising the needed funds. The feast included ten fat 'possums, five wild turkeys, and a number of

Belgian hares. [15] Sister Lloyd Blanchard, who came from Kentucky in 1883 to preside over the kitchen of Governor Eli Houston Murray, led sisters Fannie Barker, Emma Jackson, and Nellis Johnson, along with brothers Lloyd Blanchard and Andersen J. Spears, in preparing the spread. On the table was a sumptuous meal of "chicken nicely browned, yams baked in the rich gravy of the 'possum, hoe cake, tomatoes, corn that had the smoky aroma of the hills beyond the blue grass country, hot biscuits such as mother never made, coffee, and ice cream and cake." The cooks had parboiled and roasted the real ante-bellum Kentucky 'possum. The entire community of blacks and whites were invited and many turned out. The excitement of this event increased the pastor's good works and the congregation continued to grow.

Oldest Known Calvary Photo

Meanwhile, regular morning worship continued along with a 3 p.m. baptism of one of the new converts of the church on February 16, 1902. Pastor Washington's closing sermon at 8 p.m. was entitled "The World Is A Wagon Run On Four Wheels: Religion, Political, Social, Industrial."[16] With all the excitement and growth, Pastor Washington seemed to have been on a roll with his "Wagon" sermon series. They threw light upon the issues and concerns which impacted the people.

Later, instead of building a new structure, the congregation moved to 472 East 2nd South and held an opening reception at the new chapel on Sunday, June 29, 1902. In addition, members of the congregation started convening for the Alexander Dumas Literary Society on Wednesday evenings at 8:30, and for prayer meeting on Thursday evenings at 8 p.m.[17] Pastor Washington edited and published a newspaper called the *Tri-City Oracle*.[18] By early 1903, the Calvary Missionary Baptist Church officially changed the Sunday worship services to 11:00 a.m. and 7:00 p.m.[19] In 1904, the Reverend Washington died and left the Calvary field of labor to take his eternal rest. (His son, Dewey Washington, became a famous singer.)

The Alexander Dumas Literary Society

As more and more of the Calvary Missionary Baptist Church congregation became literate, they developed a keen interest in both literary and spiritual written resources. So, they came together and organized the Alexander Dumas Literary Society. This society was designed to encourage reading and discussion of ideas coming out of and related to the Black American experience. The group met regularly to exchange ideas about works they had read. Out of this practice came many of the stories and examples used to illustrate Sunday School lessons and sermons. This literary society in Salt Lake City preceded the Harlem Renaissance when African American culture was in fashion throughout the United States. It continued operating until the middle 1950s and might be considered the inspiration for poetry readings being held until now.

Changing of The Guard

As the congregation continued to meet at 472 East 2nd South with the same regular worship times, the Reverend Charles O. Boothe joined Calvary Missionary Baptist Church as their new pastor in 1904.[20] However, after a brief stay, he was replaced by the Reverend John H. Allen, under whose leadership, the congregation struggled to pay the mortgage. The 1906 Annual Report by Church Clerk, Mrs. Minerva J. Atkinson, showed a mortgage balance of $1393.00 in January 1907. Called to another church, Reverend Allen resigned and left Calvary in 1908. He moved to San Francisco, California in 1909. Mrs. Gaidy Carter served as the regular organist and choir director for the congregation.

The Calvary congregation survived for over a year (1909-1911) without a pastor but with lots of Divine help, faith, prayer, and hard work. Other changes are recorded for the Calvary Missionary Baptist Church in 1911. First, worship services were conducted at 11:00 a.m. and at 8:00 P. M. Second, Reverend William A. Magett, who lived at 735 East 800 South, is identified as the pastor.[21] He served the growing congregation until 1912. Third, the congregation secured the Eastside Baptist Church building at 679 East 300 South from the Immanuel Baptist Church and held their first service there on February 5, 1911. Fourth, a number of new families moved into the community and became members of the congregation. Several brought with them church experience. Given the pastoral instability, congregational leadership and stability depended on parishioners, individual and families, assuming leadership and providing cohesion. One example of strong lay leadership and stability at the Calvary Missionary Baptist Church is the Alice Steward family.

Calvary Missionary Baptist Church – 1911

21

The Alice Steward Family

In 1913, the Alice Sexton Steward family moved from Pueblo, Colorado to Salt Lake City, Utah. From the time of their arrival, they made a significant contribution to the community. They became active, respected, and dependable members of the Calvary Missionary Baptist Church.

Mr. Samuel Steward served faithfully on the church trustee board as well as serving as the church sexton or janitor. He supported the family by shining shoes, running the local "comfort station" on the corner of 300 South State Street near the Capital Theater, and working several other janitorial jobs. They opened their home and welcomed the children of the community. While their home was a place of discipline, safety, and spiritual nurture, those who needed help could get it at the Steward residence.

Mrs. Alice Sexton Steward, while rearing their children, gave some twelve years of respected and willing service as the beloved president of the Calvary Missionary Society. The obituary, published on December 11, 1944, reported of her, "She was truly a Christian, and raised her children in the Christian way of life. She was kind to every living creature. Flowers seemed to need only her presence to make them grow and blossom in full."[22]

Perhaps the best-known of the family was a daughter who spent most of her life here in Salt Lake and at Calvary Missionary Baptist Church. Mrs. Thelma Ruth Steward Beridon left her definite mark of the community and Calvary Missionary Baptist Church through service, community involvement, and personal dedication. For example, she assisted her father with his church janitorial duties, became the first

Alice Steward

secretary of the Salt Lake Branch National Association for the Advancement of Colored People, helped to raise funds to build and the Calvary Missionary Baptist Church.

She was, also, a leader among those who helped William and Nettie Gregory to build the Nettie Gregory Center. This center was the first and only recreation center specifically oriented toward the African-American population. When space at Calvary Missionary Baptist Church no longer met the needs for young people recreation programs, the Nettie Gregory Center was built and provided "a place to hold socials, weddings, receptions, youth oriented activities."[23] Most recently, that center housed the NAACP and the UOIC.

Another daughter, who was baptized at Calvary Missionary Baptist Church, moved away after marriage to Washington in 1933. There Mrs. Doris Steward Frye and her husband reared a son, ran a farm and operated a catering business. She returned to Salt Lake City fifty years later in 1983 to care for her ailing brother Edward. After her brother's death, Mrs. Frye volunteered to answer church office telephones, to carry out office chores, to hand out canned goods, and to distribute refreshments to Vacation Bible School participants. She gave up those duties not long before celebrating her 90th birthday in 1996. Still active and alert, she is one of the oldest members of the Calvary Missionary Baptist Church.

The Alice Steward family made a great difference on the early history of Black Baptists in Utah. They continue to make their influence felt even until now. They were a strong part of the spreading work of Black Baptists in Utah.

Tuskegee's President Booker T. Washington

Reverend Allen Newman, the next pastor, came to Calvary Missionary Baptist Church and community in 1913 and got involved in whatever he felt might improved the lot of his people. One of the most exciting things to happen during his administration was the arrangement made by Reverend Newman to have the world's best known Black leader of the time visit Calvary. In 1913, he hosted Booker T. Washington, the President of Tuskegee, Alabama Normal and Industrial Institute, perhaps the most successful American Black college at the turn of the century. Mr. Washington visited and spoke at several places while in Salt Lake City. His concluding speech on March 26, 1913 was delivered at the Calvary Missionary Baptist Church at 9:30 o'clock.[24] Writing to the editor of the New York Age, Mr. Washington wrote of the AME Utah congregation of Blacks and the Calvary Missionary Baptist Church: "They have

two good churches with very intelligent ministers."[25]

The visit of Booker T. Washington gave the African-American community much needed encouragement to continue their pioneering efforts through both Trinity African Methodist Episcopal Church and Calvary Missionary Baptist Church. The Washington self-help message and philosophy fit well with the mutual aid society, pooling of resources for sick and death benefits, approaches to church economic development.

Reverend Allen Newman

The May 30, 1914 issue of *The Western Light* newspaper, "published in the interest of the colored race," printed pictures of Calvary's recently departed Pastor Allen Newman. The paper concluded that Reverend Newman had "achieved success and fame in Salt Lake City" before moving to Northern California. It also carried pictures of the newly arrived Pastor Manasseh H. Wilkinson, a graduate of Lincoln University with highest honors, and his new wife, Señora Mae Foreman. They moved to Salt Lake City from the Shiloh Baptist Church in Williamsport, Pennsylvania.

The future for Black Baptists looked even brighter as the

reporter found the pastor to be "...the right man in the right place, being a man possessed of a disposition that at once wins for him a place in the hearts of his already many admirers." Moreover, Pastor Wilkerson's bride from Philadelphia "is noted as an elocutionist,"[26] one who practiced and taught the art of speaking. She became a popular speaker in great demand and shared her skills with others in the classroom.

The Calvary Missionary Baptist Church grew as Brothers E. Terry and P. Thomas joined the congregation on May 17, 1914. Then, Sisters Barnes and Tucker became members on May 24, 1914. The choir was reorganized under the leadership of Brother E. Watts so that its members could sing both morning and night, which had never been done before. The Reverend Wilkerson preached two powerful sermons on May 31, 1914, one in the morning entitled "Christian Boldness" and a second in the evening entitled "Going Home." His reputation and career in Salt Lake City was clearly established for all who heard his messages.

Pastor Wilkerson was outgoing, with a pleasant personality. He had little trouble establishing rapport. In fact, he generated such a spirit of brotherhood with Protestant churches in the area that he started the soon-to-be common practice of choir and pulpit exchanges. This activity engaged congregations of Blacks as well as whites.

Reverend Manasseh Wilkerson & Mrs. Senora M. Wilkerson

Between 1914 and 1916, Sunday School attendance at Calvary Missionary Baptist Church ranged from four to fourteen while the collections never were more than eighty-four cents. The church heating system presented major problems. Sister Thelma

Ruth Steward and other Sunday School participants had to make a fire before Sunday School in order that the building would be warm enough for the later worship services. (The Steward family had recently moved to Salt Lake City from Colorado.) After some initial growth under Reverend Wilkerson's leadership, the congregation seemed to stall in both membership and raising money for financial obligations. The people just could not stretch their resources any further. So, two years after his arrival, Reverend Wilkerson delivered his farewell lecture not to the morning worship group but to the Sunday School on April 16, 1916.

He then moved to Omaha, Nebraska to continue his ministry.

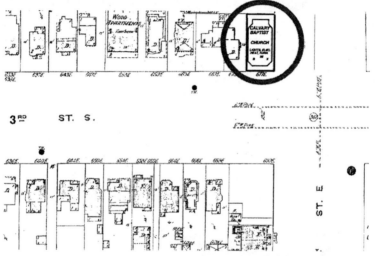

Calvary Baptist Church

The Northern Baptist Association

The Calvary Missionary Baptist Church continued without a pastor until August 1916. The congregation called the Reverend George W. Hart(s) from the practice of law to serve as their pastor. He was excited about the potential for outreach and fellowship with other local congregations as well as the need for some sort of national connections. By December 1917, Reverend Hart(s) had succeeded in getting Calvary more formally and actively involved with the Northern Baptist Association. This body, which had been organized in the area during October 1884 and was growing, consisted mostly of congregations of White Baptist.

The Northern Baptist Association changed its name to the American Baptist Association. It made its initial impact on Black Baptist by providing financial assistance which guaranteed Calvary's pastor a regular salary for the first time. When Pastor Hart(s) departed as Calvary split and the congregation met for worship in a union hall on Post Office Street, the association helped in two ways. First, they invited the congregation to return to the 679 East 300 South building for worship services. Second, they supplied visiting ministers to conduct worship services while the congregation was without a pastor.

However, the Northern Baptist Association's attempt to place a Reverend Brannon as permanent pastor of Calvary failed completely in 1922. For the predominately Black congregation did not want a pastor from another racial background. Operating with congregational government, attitudes and distinctions about skin color were serious considerations. Details about this concern are discussed below.

The Blue Vein Society

One of the sources of problems within the congregation during the second and third decade of the 1900s had to do with attitudes of members toward each other. This clear indication that the church was unable to escape the social practices of its time, particularly those related to intra racial conflicts and differentiation, is provided by the seating arrangements. Sadly, attendants to church activities separated and seated themselves according to their skin color. Those with light-skin and straight hair sat on one side while those with darker skin sat on the opposite side. One group had little or nothing to do with the other, especially in social gatherings.

In fact, those of one skin tone seemed to get along better with those of the same skin tone from the AME congregation than they did with those with a different hue within Calvary. The success, the length of service tenure, and the day-to-day harmony depended on whether the pastor was part of the majority or not. Commonly practiced in various African American communities across the USA, this intra racial stratification, validating and valorizing the lightness of one's skin which allowed the blood to be seen through the veins, was called the "Blue Bloods" or the "Blue Vein Society." The Charles McSwine and the Guy Overall families instigated this custom at Calvary. The early group consisted of between 20 and 30 people. They thought they were better than other Blacks perhaps because they were more accepted outside the Black community.

The oldest member of Calvary Missionary Baptist Church in 1996 came with her family to the church in 1913. She was about six years old. In 1920, at the age of 13, Sister Doris Steward (later Frye) joined the church when Evangelist Skipworth led a revival. She was baptized by Pastor Hart. Although she married and moved away, she returned to care for her brother and, now, volunteers to work in the church office and kitchen.

According to Sister Frye, who experienced growing up during those days, the "Blue Vein Society" members thought they were better than others. They limited their association and socialization to those looking most like themselves. On one occasion, some of them created quite a stir within the Steward family. They said to the teenage Doris Frye, "When you get old enough, you're going to be one of us, too." Mr. and Mrs. Steward were upset because members of their family would have fit into both groups. So, the real problem with this practice was that it divided families,[27] and the people allowed the practice to come between them.

Summary

From its inception, the Calvary Missionary Baptist Church saw itself as a beacon in the Salt Lake valley. Her goal was to provide spiritual guidance for Black Baptists in Utah. Beginning as the near flickering efforts of a handful of women, she eventually grew into a glowing congregation by the second decade of this century. The Calvary Missionary Baptist Church became the community center for "colored" youth from about 1913 until the late 1920s. According to Sister Mary Smith, "...I went to the Baptist Church, because all the kids went to the Baptist Church. You know, that's where you got to see everybody on Sunday. I was the only colored girl in the school."[28] For African-Americans, the Church has always been a safe haven, a natural gathering place.

The Calvary Missionary Baptist Church strengthened and developed people spiritually, raised funds for building and operational expenses, dealt with issues, bought buildings, sponsored leaders, and, in short, blossomed through appreciation and respect. She made every effort to demonstrate that "love that runs from heart to heart and from breast to breast so that we can all feel one another's care." Her leaders were creative, energetic, and skillful. These humble beginnings rest on a foundation of strong preaching and effective example setting. Although *The Broad Ax* moved to Chicago in 1899, the *Plain Dealer* publisher died in 1907, and the *Tri-City Oracle* was short-lived, the Calvary Missionary Baptist Church remained alive and well. Perhaps the Biblical foundation, the fellowship of people, and the leadership responsibilities accepted by Black Baptists helped the congregations to survive and flourish while other institutions demised. As a single congregation, Calvary shined her light and sang with conviction: "This Little Light Of Mine I'm Going To Let It Shine."

Chapter 2
The Scattering Brotherhood

For more than two decades (22 years), the Calvary Missionary Baptist Church was essentially the one and only congregation of Black Baptists in Utah. Her viability and visibility were enhanced in part by the business relationship and/or arrangement she established with the Northern Baptist Church, now known as the American Baptist Church, as early as November 1910, after many years of experiencing the ups and downs of a sole pioneering congregation. This initial commitment involved a $500.00 gift Calvary received from The American Baptist Home Mission Society (The Society). That gift would have to "be repaid by this Church, provided this Church does not comply with, or violates its covenants and agreements and the conditions..." Ninety percent of Calvary's congregation voted in favor of the resolution and Mrs. Lena Dallas, the church clerk, signed the instrument documenting this transaction.[29]

The Society made loans to both "colored" and white congregations of Baptist churches, as well as missions, to promote the preaching of the gospel, to establish, maintain, and aid them, and to make acquisition of sites to erect worship houses. In addition, The Society provided ministerial personnel and financial support to a number of these congregations. In Utah, Calvary Missionary Baptist Church was not the only beneficiary. The Society was also instrumental in the establishing of the Wall Avenue Baptist Church, which was started in 1916 in Ogden, Utah. That congregation of Black Baptists still operates today and is known as New Zion Baptist Church.

Wall Avenue (New Zion) Baptist Church

In 1918, as Wall Avenue Baptist congregation continued to grow, the Utah Baptist State Convention purchased a lot for $1100.00, and a building was constructed some time later by the congregation.[30] Utah corporation records show that Wall Avenue Baptist Church was officially incorporated on Christmas day 1926. For some years, the congregation survived first one challenge then another. Forty years later, led by Reverend Benjamin J. Washington, the church raised funds and with more than 50,000 hours of volunteer labor constructed a new church house. The congregation moved from Wall Avenue to 2935 Lincoln Avenue. The name was changed to New Zion Baptist Church and the new building was dedicated debt-free during the week of October 19 through 26, 1958. The congregation continues to serve the spiritual needs of Black Baptists living in Ogden in 1996.

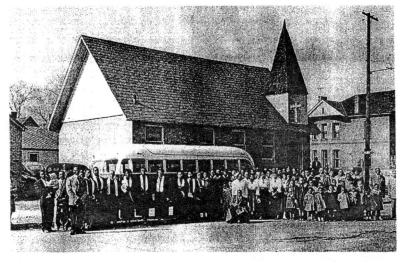

Wall Avenue Baptist Church

31

Contingent Mortgages

Although there is no record of these early Black churches taking a vote to be affiliated with the American Baptist Convention, they worked cooperatively. For example, Calvary Missionary Baptist Church agreed to purchase the Eastside Baptist Church building located at the corner of 700 East and 300 South from The Society. On June 20, 1921, The Society issued a deed to the Calvary Missionary Baptist Church. The Society and the Congregation agreed upon a $2500.00 contingent mortgage on August 30, 1921. The Reverend George W. Hart(s) signed as president, on behalf of the congregation. On September 11, 1929, that contingent mortgage was later transferred to the Utah State Baptist Convention church edifice work project, the business of providing funds for the construction and maintenance of church facilities. The document identified the church occupying the property as "Calvary (col'd) Baptist Church, SLC."

Consequently, Calvary Missionary Baptist Church leased the facility for $1.00 per year until they built another structure in the middle 1960s. When Calvary vacated the building, the structure was sold to the Lagoon company. The building was moved and renovated it in 1966. Two years later, on January 9, 1968, the land was sold for $7428.00 to C & I Realty Profit Sharing Trust.[31] The lot remains vacant until the present time.

Similarly, the June 8, 1925-mortgage of $200.00 on the Wall Avenue Baptist Church of Ogden was assigned, transferred and delivered to The Society by agreement on October 4, 1928.[32] The Society, also, paid the salary or portions of the salary for Wall Avenue Baptist Church's pastor from April 11, 1925 until May 12, 1942.[33] Thus, the Black Baptist congregations of Calvary and Wall Avenue were assisted by the Utah Baptist State Convention from their early beginnings until the middle 1960s.

Birth of New Congregations

With increasing numbers of Blacks working in the mines and for the railroad, the Sunnyside Baptist Church was established in Carbon County in 1919. Names and additional information about any pastors, leaders or members of this congregation are not available. Unfortunately, the congregation continued for a very, very short duration. As the community residents were very mobile, congregational leadership as well as members were constantly moving to maintain work.

For similar reasons, in 1922, the First Baptist Church congregation was started in Mohrland, Utah. In 1923, Reverend M. H. Flemmings served as Vice-Moderator of the Utah, Idaho and Wyoming Baptists Association and pastor of the First Baptist congregation of Mohrland, Utah. Many spiritual needs were met, but the church closed in 1927.

The Pilgrim Baptist Church was established in Salt Lake City on May 16, 1922 at the home of Mr. and Mrs. Angus Pickett and incorporated on November 8, 1927. This congregation experienced numerous changes including destruction by fire in October 1948. Yet, the members continue to rally and the congregation holds light of Christian faith in 1996. The Pilgrim Baptist Church sought recognition at the Sixth Annual Session of the Utah, Idaho and Wyoming Baptists Association held on August 16, 1923. By resolution of the Association, "The Pilgrim Baptist Church of Salt Lake City would be recognized after the members of that church had received their letters from the Calvary Baptist Church."[34]

The Salt Lake Branch NAACP

Reverend George W. Hart(s) had come to pastor Calvary Missionary Baptist Church well-prepared for the leadership demands that would come upon him in Utah. For example, when a group of soldiers committed an act of brutality against a group of young ladies from Calvary, Reverend Hart(s) organized Salt

Lake City's chapter of the National Association for the Advancement of Colored People (NAACP) on February 10, 1919, just ten years after the parent body was organized in New York. He became the first president of the local chapter of this civil rights organization. Thelma Steward became its first secretary.

Today, the Salt Lake Branch National Association For the Advancement of Colored People remains very active and strong in Salt Lake City. Many of Calvary Missionary Baptist Church's current members hold leadership positions. In fact, past presidents, Mr. Johnny M. Driver, Mr. James Dooley and Mrs. Alberta Henry, as well as the current president, Mrs. Jeanetta Williams, were or are members of Calvary Missionary Baptist Church. Continuing her role in leadership during October 1995, Calvary's congregation became the first Utah church to purchase a fully paid life membership in the civil rights organization.

The Utah, Idaho, and Wyoming Baptist Association

In 1917, Reverend George W. Hart(s) called together the Missionary Baptist Church congregations in the three state area and organized the Utah, Idaho and Wyoming Baptists Association. According to the bylaws and adopted constitution, the object of this association was "to promote the preaching of the gospel and establish churches in destitute places, at home, and abroad."[35] The association exercised no ecclesiastical authority over member churches and could not "meddle with the internal affairs" of any congregation.[36] Membership in the Association was open to any and all "regular Missionary Baptist Churches and any members of Missionary Baptist Churches in good standing." Congregations "found sound in the Faith and accepting the Doctrine of the Baptist Church" joined with a letter and twenty-five cents per member each of four yearly sessions. Individuals registered "by paying $1.00 annually or $3.00 for life members.[37]

The Association held quarterly sessions. The first annual session was held with the Wall Avenue Baptist Church, August 20-24, 1918.[38]

Each annual session would include at least three sermons, one dealing with doctrine, one emphasizing the importance of both religious and secular education, and one on self-control or temperance.[39] At the Sixth Annual Session, held again with the Wall Avenue Baptist Church on August 16-19, 1923, new congregations were received as members. They included the Second Baptist Church of Idaho Falls, Idaho, under the leadership of the Reverend G. S. Stacker; and the First Baptist Church of Mohrland, Utah, pastored by the Reverend M. H. Flemmings. In addition, the Pilgrim Baptist Church of Salt Lake City, Utah, was received on condition that her members return to Calvary Missionary Baptist Church and receive their letters.[40] (This congregation emerged in 1922 when Pastor Hart(s) along with thirty-one members split off and left Calvary over issues related to the newly organized association.) The official annual committee of the Utah, Idaho and Wyoming Baptists Association consisted of Reverend George W. Hart(s), Reverend A. J. Billingsly, C. O. Smith, Sister Fanny M. Jackson, and Sister Dixon.

Articles of Incorporation

On May 11, 1921, brother William L. Johnson chaired a meeting in which the Calvary Missionary Baptist Church congregation adopted Articles of Incorporation. The church became a corporation of the state of Utah for the purpose of worshiping God and providing instructions in Christian religion.

The first board consisted of George W. Hart(s) (president), Matrina Johnson (clerk), Minerva J. Atkinson (treasurer), William

Gregory, William F. Burgess, James Hamilton, Joseph Brown, and James S. True. They were to hold office until January 1, 1922 or until their respective successors were elected and qualified. Secretary of State Hyrum E. Crockett issued the Certificate of Incorporation on May 19, 1921, for the Calvary Missionary Baptist Church of Salt Lake City, Utah.

After Pastor Hart(s) departed, it took quiet some time but a new pastor was eventually selected and, with Sister Emma (Mom Jack) Jackson chairing the committee, a formal installation and reception with printed invitations was held for the Reverend J. D. Wilson of Tennessee on August 8, 1923. Dr. E. W. Moore of New York traveled to Salt Lake as guest of the congregation and delivered the installation address. This event demonstrated the connections between Calvary Missionary Baptist Church and other National Baptist Churches across the country The deacon board included J. N. Nance (chairman), C. T. Smith, Humphrey Means, and H. W. Osborne. Sister Fanny M. Jackson served as church clerk. Due to serious domestic problems, the Reverend Wilson's term as pastor was short-lived and he resigned in 1925 when domestic problems overwhelmed him and his ministry.

A White Pastor Serving Black Baptist

Between 1926 and 1929, the Reverend Mack Stovall, a white minister, pastored the Calvary Missionary Baptist Church by mutual consent of the congregation and the predominately white Northern Baptist Association. A number of programmatic changes were made in the order of services, as Sister Beulah Guinn, the church clerk (also the mother of the Harlem Renaissance writer Wallace Thurman, who was born in and attended Calvary Missionary Baptist Church of Salt Lake City)[41], indicated in her 1927 annual report. Sunday School was changed from 12:30 P. M. to 10:00 a.m. to allow the morning worship services to commence at 11:00 A. M. The same report speaks of Brother William Gregory's ordination as a deacon on May 21, 1926. Sisters Mignon Barker Richmond and Ella Louise DeBies are identified as active members of the congregation during this year. Zelmar R. Lawrence and Henry Nathaniel, both Black students studying at the University of Utah, were among the young college age participants in the church Easter program presented by The Young Folks Dramatic Club.[42]

Ella Louise DeBies

Sister Ella Louise DeBies, affectionately known as "Mother DeBies," was born on October 11, 1891 and came to Calvary Missionary Baptist Church in 1927. She served faithfully until her death on January 6, 1985. For more than 50 years, she was always present and served as deaconess, choir member, and missionary society worker. The secret of her well-spent life was an unwavering faith in God, the willingness to help others, faithful participation in the local Church, liberal giving, and firm principles to live by. Reverend France A. Davis remembers that she provided him with the support and trust as he built his ministry at Calvary Missionary Baptist Church in Utah.

Mignon Barker Richmond

A second long term member of the Calvary Missionary Baptist Church was Sister Mignon B. Richmond. She was born April 1, 1897 in Salt Lake City. Her service at the church included being Sunday School superintendent and chairman of the Trustee Board. She took her influence outside of the church to the larger community and was effective in community organizing. In her honor, Salt Lake City designated a park behind her house as "Mignon B. Richmond Park" in 1986 and Utah State University named a multi cultural and scholarship society to honor her as their first African-American graduate in 1992. She made a tremendous difference in the educational, community organizing, and spiritual growth of this community.

William Gregory

A third individual making a difference in the Black Baptist community was Brother William Gregory who arrived in Salt Lake City in 1913. He worked both for the railroad and as a shoe shine man. When the Calvary Missionary Baptist Church got into trouble, it was ofttimes Brother Gregory who came to the rescue. On at least one occasion, he assumed the mortgage on the church parsonage until the congregation could return his money. He served as a deacon and helped to build the Nettie Gregory Community Center which still exists today. He said of the work he and his wife Nettie did, "There just wasn't much wholesome recreation for the young folks down here on the west side back then. So we started some programs at the Calvary Baptist Church."[43]

Despite the requisite growing pains, these were indeed exciting days for the Calvary Missionary Baptist Church of Salt Lake City, Wall Avenue Baptist Church of Ogden, Sunnyside Baptist Church of Carbon County, First Baptist Church of Mohrland, and Pilgrim Baptist Church of Salt Lake City. These five Baptist congregations were made up of predominately Black members located across the state of Utah. They worked together as members of the Utah, Idaho and Wyoming Baptists Association. They divided to multiply and split to unite.

Summary

The second phase of Black Baptists Church life is Utah became more formal. The interactions between various bodies, through larger civic and religious organizations, made possible some task individual congregations could not accomplish. Several individuals and families contributed and left lasting tributes to themselves and the community. A new day was dawning for those who choose to worship as Black Baptists in Utah. That which started as but one flickering star soon spread to glow like the morning sun.

Chapter 3
Those Who Overcome

With the number of congregations increasing, some Black Baptist congregations sprung up in Utah out of need but dwindled for lack of support. Others struggled to get started, died temporarily, and sprang up again. Still, others managed to hang on and keep the doors open for worship. Perhaps the greatest difficulty was lack of money. Describing the economic conditions and individual buying power, Leo Oliver, who was baptized into the Calvary Missionary Baptist Church in 1919, observed, "My father...worked all day and half the night for $27.50 a month....Back then, things were different. I remember I used to post a first class letter for two cents, a postcard, one cent. I bought me a 1928 Chevrolet four-door sedan for $450.00. You can't hardly get tires for that nowadays."[44]

Mary Rucker

The churches collected what resources they could and used them to survive during trying times. Offerings were sometimes no more than a few pennies, and whenever they collected $20.00, they considered it a windfall. They reached out for help to other groups while organizing themselves to be more efficient. New pastors were called into the area with better training and more experience. The congregations that survived remained stable in spite of the great economic depression and World War II.

Financial Challenges

As these congregations existed within their respective socioeconomic communities, they faced the same challenges as the larger communities. Often, church offerings did not amount to very much and some people could only give of their crops and from their gardens. Many pastors remember their only pay as fresh fruit, vegetables, and a piece of meat. Consequently, most congregations turned to a variety of fund raising efforts. They included pew rallies, musicals with guest choirs and a special soloist, men and women days, and homecoming day celebrations. Many of these efforts pitted one group in competition against another to see who could raise the largest amount of money. Church auxiliaries and departments worked hard to meet certain quotas. Ofttimes, as was true of the 1902 'Possum Feast, these fund raising events involved many hours of hard work around a hot stove, cooking cakes, pies, and meals of ribs, chicken, and chitterlings.

To deal with some of the economic needs, the Reverend Charles Spencer, who was called to the ministry and studied The Bible while in prison, established and directed a free employment bureau for Negroes in Salt Lake City during his tenure as pastor of the Calvary congregation from 1932 until 1941. His daughter Elect and her husband E. B. Daniels operated the Daniels' Elect Barber and Beauty Salon at 211 East 700 South. This was the first licensed shop of its kind in the state of Utah.[45]

Financially, the 1930s and 1940s were extremely difficult for all of these Black Baptist congregations. For example, the Calvary Missionary Baptist Church bargained to purchase a parsonage at 634 South 700 East. To keep up with the burdensome payments, the parsonage was rented. Still, The Reverend Spencer and the congregation could not meet the mortgage obligations without extra help. Associate Minister, the Reverend Humphrey Means assumed the mortgage payments and Calvary was never able to reclaim the property. Later, the Reverend William A. Lucas led the congregation to purchase a second parsonage, which was sold for delinquent taxes in 1945. The congregation redeemed the property in that same year and mortgaged it again for $800.00. During the same time period, the building required a new heating system for which the congregation did not have the money. Trustees Robert Lewis and George James agreed to make the payments with the stipulation that the amount paid would be credited to their church dues. God seemed to have always had "a ram in the thicket" or a "way out of no way."

The Reverend W. L. Holloway and his wife, Jesse, came to Calvary in April 1948. The congregation agreed to pay him $100.00 per month along with $1.25 per week for bus fare. To secure the needed resources, the new pastor introduced the congregation to pledge cards, called the congregation to vote that all auxiliaries turn half of the money collected over to the general treasurer, and divided the membership into "tribes" as a system to receive church dues.[46] The "tribe" system worked very well with Brother Daley E. Oliver as chairman and Sisters Thelma Beridon, Lutie Morgan, Ella Louise DeBies, and Sattie Etherly and Brothers David H. Oliver as the first captains. This tribal system served to remind the congregation of their African heritage while providing a familiar organization for fund raising.. Working alongside the regular church organizations was The Progressive Women's Club, made up of Calvary members. In 1950, this club cleaned and painted the church kitchen then installed a new stove and refrigerator provided by Sister Linnie Wells.

Similar difficulties were experienced by our sister congregations. For example, with only one congregation continuing to meet the needs of Black Baptists in Ogden, pastors were coming and going. In 1948, the Reverend J. L. Rollerson of Denver, Colorado was called by the 100 member congregation and served well until called home from labor to reward by death on Sunday afternoon December 2, 1951. The congregation had grown by nearly fifty percent to 143 members when Pastor Rollerson died. Perhaps the greatest pastoral change of Wall Avenue Baptist's history came when the Reverend Benjamin J. Washington preached his first sermon as pastor on May 1, 1952. He came with a vision to purchase a new parsonage and build a new church immediately. Two months after his arrival, a new parsonage was purchased and furnished for $8000.00.[47] Pastor Washington joined the Western States Missionary Baptist Convention and soon became one of its leading participants and supporters.

Sunnyside House Church Becomes Helper House Church

When the Davison family moved from Oklahoma to Sunnyside in 1941, there was no church to worship in. The people lived in a mining camp among the tumbleweed and sagebrush. The only public buildings in the community were the post office, the company store, the pool hall and the drug store. So, Black Baptists in those surrounding coal mining communities met for worship in various homes. According to Mrs. Anna Davison Whitehorn Morris who grew up in the area, the house of Mr. Isaiah Walker became the most common meeting place in Sunnyside. Deacons and others conducted Sunday School each week and led in prayer meeting on Wednesday, especially during World War II. In 1945 or 1946, Mr. Walker secured a little house rent and utility free from the Utah Fuel Company, owners of the local mining operation as a place of worship.

"Eventually, the group started meeting in Helper and various ministers from Salt Lake City and Ogden would come to help the people. The Reverend Ira L. Martin stayed longest and did the most for the congregation. These ministers would arrive on Saturday, spend the night in family homes, lead the Sunday worship, and depart Sunday afternoon. The families fed and took care of the needs of the visiting ministers who came to Helper. A majority of the people who attended the services came from Sunnyside to Helper. [48]

"Fund raising for the Helper congregation involved a number creative efforts. These included a "Chitterlings and Bean Strut" which consisted of an individual walking down the aisle with chitterlings and beans on a knife without dropping them. Participants enrolled with a donation. Any person who dropped the chitterlings or beans would be disqualified and those who did not would receive a prize. A second effort was the "apron sale." Then married to Mr. Whitehorn, I was a good seamstress and made all of the aprons sold. A third fund raising event was the "picnic basket auctions." The men would bid on decorated baskets or boxes of food prepared and wrapped by the women. The winner would not only get to eat the food but would have the opportunity to spend time with the women as well. I had become a great cook and baked cakes as well as prepared meals for many of the bachelors in the area.

Single men seldom came to worship or other church events but they always gave money when asked. Regardless of what may have taken place the night before, the married men would bring their families to church and would sit outside in the car. Mr. Ted Harris, who owned and operated a "good time house," was known as "the man with the money" and he was always the most generous contributor in church fund raising efforts.[49]

Church On Fire

There is a familiar story about a boy who stood outside as a church building burned. When asked why nobody had seen him there before, he responded, "I have never seen the church on fire before." That was the general reaction when a tragic fire destroyed the building of the Pilgrim Baptist Church in Salt Lake City. After the Reverend Jesse Killings became pastor of Pilgrim Baptist Church in August 1947, the church building burned down in October 1948 and for four years the congregation did not have a permanent place of worship. They met from house to house until a new church was completed in April 1952. Despite the circumstances, the church continued as if it were an unquenchable flame. Subsequently, with the construction of a new interstate freeway, in 1955, the church was forced to relocate. Reverend Louis D. Williams led the congregation to build the new facility on three acres of land at 1624 South 1000 West. With a new facility,

Pilgrim Baptist Church
SLC – 1947

the church changed its name to the New Pilgrim Baptist Church and celebrated with a victory march on Sunday June 7, 1959 at 3:00 p.m.[50]

Military Support Ministry

With a large proportion of their membership being military related and away from their families, the Black Baptist churches saw their need. This clearly indicated that it was time to reach out into the community to render services beyond the church walls. For example, during the World War II era, both Calvary Missionary Baptist Church and Pilgrim Baptist Church cooperated with the Trinity AME and the YWCA to encourage and welcome returning veterans. They hosted a banquet led by Mrs. Marguerite Browne and Mrs. Thelma Beridon on March 22, 1946.[51] These three congregations paid special attention to those returning soldiers sick and injured at the Veteran's Hospital and others assigned to Camp Kearns. Local business owners who were affiliated with these churches went the extra mile to do their part, too. For example, MOMS (Mrs. Hampton, proprietor of the New J. H. Hotel) provided "a home away from home" and was like a mother for many members of the WAC. At the same time, all the military personnel found a warm welcome and meals of steak and fried chicken at the Porters and Waiters Cafe operated by C. H. Wright.

The Rocky Mountain Baptist Association

By July 12, 1944, the Association of Black Baptist Churches had changed its name to the Rocky Mountain Baptist Association. It included congregations from the four states of Utah, Idaho, Wyoming, and Montana. The Tenth Annual Session of the Association convened at the Second Baptist Church in Cheyenne, Wyoming. Reverend William A. Lucas of Calvary Missionary Baptist Church in Salt Lake City served as moderator, Reverend William I. Monroe of Cheyenne's Second Baptist Church as first vice moderator, Reverend W. H. Hicks as second vice moderator of Bethel Baptist Church in Pocatello, Idaho, and Reverend J. L. Conner of Ogden's Wall Avenue Baptist Church as treasurer.

New Pilgrim Baptist Church – Salt Lake City

Moderator Lucas said in his annual address, "This is the first assembly we have had comprised of the whole body of the Association since 1942... Our Association now includes four states: Utah, Idaho, Wyoming, and Montana. It is our desire that the Association will grow indefinitely throughout the Rocky Mountains." He continued his vision for the area, "It is my plan to see that we bring the whole district under control, and at such points as seem advisable I plan to establish mission stations. Our biggest job is to secure a minister whom we can put on the field as full time missionary. I am praying that we can increase our financial standing to the extent that we can bear the full expenses of such a missionary. At the present I am asking that each pastor do what he can to contact and keep alive such missions points as are in his own state until we can get a permanent missionary."[52]

The Annual Sermon was delivered by Reverend M. H. Houston of Casper, Wyoming from the text John 11:28. His theme for the informative and inspiring sermon was: "Making Religion Work."[53] The missionary sermon by Reverend J. L. Conner gave clear directions under the title, "What Does God Ask Of Us?" As public accommodations were not open to Blacks, delegates for the Wednesday through Friday session of the Rocky Mountain Baptist Association slept in private homes of church members and enjoyed their well-cooked meals. It was a time of rich renewal and spiritual sharing for all who attended.

Having served previously as the pastor of Pilgrim Baptist Church of Salt Lake City, the Reverend William A. Lucas had come back from Washington to assume the leadership of Calvary Missionary Baptist Church. His operational motto was: "A Church With

Deacon Ray and
Sister Clydies Finn

A Vision and A Minister With A Message." He not only served as pastor of the Calvary Missionary Baptist Church, but also as moderator of the Rocky Mountain Baptist Association, Incorporated. That Association of Black Baptist churches set about training and organizing both laymen and clergy.

In the February 13-14, 1946 session, Moderator Lucas brought a powerful sermon admonishing all on the subject: "Straighten Up and Fly Right."[54] Another speaker talked to clergy and lay leaders about "On Raising The Church Budget Through A Small Congregation." The association tried to meet the spiritual needs of Black Baptists throughout the Rocky Mountain area while struggling to meets its own economic requirements. Leadership of the Association rotated among the various member congregations so that each one felt included.

The Rocky Mountain Messenger

Furthermore, the Reverend Lucas found time to edit and publish a monthly magazine called *The Rocky Mountain Messenger*. In it, he shared information about the work of Black Baptist churches and related institutions. The publication began monthly publication with the October 1945 magazine. Copies were available for 25 cents each or $2.50 per yearly subscription. Papers were available to Black Baptists congregations, the African-American community at large, and the entire Salt Lake City area. This attractive magazine publicized and broadened the influence of the Black Baptist churches, especially Calvary Missionary Baptist Church. The

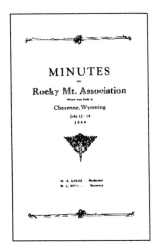

Rocky Mountain Association Minutes

Church and the magazine outlined and promoted the "welfare of the church and the community."[55]

Articles in the magazine sought to clarify doctrinal issues as well as to celebrate seasonal holidays such as Christmas and Easter. Some short tidbits of gossip were reported but never without suggestions being offered for appropriate behavior. These tidbits dealt with such things as who would be marrying, who had not been seen in church lately, and how not to treat your pastor. Poems by various writers were also shared for the readers to consider. Volumes of *The Rocky Mountain Messenger* identified officers and departments of the churches. Public events and programs were announced and publicized, such as the 1946 Rocky Mountain Baptist Conference of Ministers and Laymen. The Utah Baptist Ministers organization held a retreat in Ogden on January 10-11, 1946, using the theme, "The Christian Church For Our Day." The Reverend Lucas served as president of the group and adjourned the meeting after much deliberation by sharing in communion.

One particular article included the address with advice from the Reverend Lucas to ministers invited to fill pulpits for pastors on leave. The article advised, "Visiting Preachers Should Not Meddle In The Church."[56] Individual churches operated schools of religion designed to foster religious education through teaching, training, and missions for both leaders and followers. In no sense of the word did Black Baptists concern themselves only with the business of preaching. Instead, they took seriously the need and call for educational and social ministry with the goal of making a positive difference is every area where people hurt.

Summary

The third and fourth decades of the twentieth century made great demands on Black Baptists in Utah. Many of the efforts of existing congregations were limited by the great economic depression. Emerging congregations sought to fill some of the gaps within their own communities. Young, hardworking, and formally educated families moved into Utah to make a better life for themselves as well as others. They became contributing members of the various Black Baptists congregations. In spite of the hardships, congregations united with each other and refused to let the light of hope be extinguished.

Chapter 4
Spreading the Light

From the earliest days of 1892 until 1954, there were five different Black congregations of Baptists organized in Utah. The Sunnyside Baptist Church of Carbon County and the First Baptist Church of Mohrland experienced only a very short life. However, the Calvary Missionary Baptist Church of Salt Lake City, the Wall Avenue Baptist Church of Ogden, and the Pilgrim Baptist Church of Salt Lake City weathered numerous economic storms and survived as viable congregations. All three continue to provide spiritual leadership in the 1990s. Both those which did not continue for long and those which live on worked together as members of the Utah, Idaho, and Wyoming Baptists Association. United, they faced and overcame numerous economic, social, and spiritual obstacles to provide a sense of community and a haven of worship.

Later, as the separate-but-equal doctrine and practice was ruled unconstitutional by the Brown v. Topeka, Kansas Board of Education United States Supreme Court decision, additional changes occurred within the Utah's Black Baptist congregations. The Wall Avenue Baptist congregation purchased a new parsonage with two lots for a new edifice on February 15, 1954 for $9850.00 They held ground breaking services on May 16, 1954 where Mr. Obie Blackmore, an usher, donated $100.00 to match the less than $100.00 already in the church bank account.[57] As the hymn proclaims, "The Lord will Make a Way, Somehow."

New Hope Baptist Church of Salt Lake City

One of the great things to happen was the organizing of New Hope Missionary Baptist Church of Salt Lake City on November

17, 1954 by Reverend Jesse Killings. Reverend Killings was elected pastor and twenty names were placed on the church membership roll. During the organization meeting, the congregation petitioned God to make them "A Living Church, a Working Church, whose major purpose was the Saving of Souls."[58] The church opened her doors at 517 South Second East on December 12, 1954 and, later, the congregation occupied facilities between 800 South and 900 South on 200 West (829 South 200 West). Other pastors of this third Salt Lake City congregation included Reverend A. N. Conley, Reverend Ira L. Martin, Reverend M. H. Washington, Reverend F. D Brown, Reverend James Gates, and Reverend Isaac P. Brantley.

Reverend Lester R. Agent

As the membership declined, the congregation managed to keep the doors open until the disbanding of the church in 1977 after the resignation of Reverend Isaac P. Brantley. The members transferred to Calvary Missionary Baptist, New Pilgrim Baptist, and Shiloh Baptist. Funds from the sale of property and facilities were divided one-fourth to Calvary Missionary Baptist Church, one-fourth to New Pilgrim Baptist, one-fourth to Shiloh Baptist, and one-fourth to the Alberta Henry Education Scholarship Fund. This distribution of funds acknowledged the churches which received some of the New Hope members and the importance of continued support of the scholarship fund.

Two years or so after the New Hope congregation began in Salt Lake City, a second Pilgrim Baptist Church started meeting in various Helper, Utah homes. Among the pastors serving this congregation in a mining and railroad community were Reverend Ira L. Martin, Reverend George Harris, and Reverend Douglas A. Washington. However, as mining slowed and the railroad became less dominate in the transportation business, the church facilities were abandoned and eventually sold in the late 1970s. By this time, a majority of the members had moved away to Salt Lake City and other places. The few that remained in the area found other ways and places to get their needs satisfied.

Gift Mortgages

Both the Calvary Missionary Baptist Church of Salt Lake City and the Wall Avenue Baptist Church of Ogden occupied facilities under a gift mortgage arrangement with the American Baptist. The American Baptist Home Mission Society held the $2500.00 mortgage on Calvary and the $200.00 mortgage on Wall Avenue from 1921 and 1925 respectively. In 1954, Calvary under the pastorate of Reverend William I. Monroe leased the property for $1.00 per year.[59] These arrangements required no repayment of the mortgage unless and until the congregations ceased to function as congregations of Baptists.

These were difficult times for the congregations of Black Baptists, financially and otherwise. For example, Calvary bargained to purchase a parsonage but could not make the payments and keep up with their

Alberta Henry and Lois Conner

ongoing and regular upkeep bills at the same time. At first, the parsonage was rented out, later mortgaged, and eventually lost through foreclosure when the congregation could not raise the funds needed.

The Wall Avenue Baptist church became the New Zion Baptist Church of Ogden and their new facilities at 2935 Lincoln Avenue were constructed with the sweat and labor of Reverend Benjamin J. Washington and many hours of volunteer labor. The Pilgrim Baptist Church had burned down on 300 South and 700 West during 1946. The congregation continued to meet from place to place until a new building was built by Reverend Benjamin J. Washington and it became known as the New Pilgrim Baptist Church at 1626 South 1000 West in Salt Lake City.

Reorganized Utah-Idaho Baptist Association

Not only was Reverend Benjamin J. Washington busy as a pastor and builder, but he called the congregations of Blacks together and reorganized them into the Utah-Idaho Baptist Association in 1955. Early membership in this reorganized association included the Bethel Baptist Church and Corinth Baptist Church in Pocatello, Idaho, the Pilgrim Baptist Church in Helper, Utah, the New Zion Baptist Church in Ogden, and the Calvary Missionary Baptist Church, New Hope Missionary Baptist Church, and New Pilgrim Baptist Church of Salt Lake City, Utah. The congregations worked closely with each other to achieve missionary and educational goals while developing active affiliations with other regional and national bodies. Pooling resources and consolidating effort made the work easier.

Calvary Baptist Church – 1954

In 1956, the Youth Department of the Association was organized with Sister Ethel Washington of New Zion Baptist Church as director. Other adult directors which followed included Janet Twiggs Martin, Tommie Ellis Watkins, Virgia Wilder, SheWanda Offord Robertson, Michelle Boyd, Dula Brock, and Patricia Gray. Youth presidents of the Department have included Gloria Green, Sandy Hutchinson, Olwyn Wilder, Adrienne Dorby, Anthony L. Carpenter, and Taedra Morris.

With the close relationship between Reverend Benjamin J. Washington and Reverend Milton K. Curry and because Reverend Washington had served as president of the Western States Missionary Baptist Convention, the association and local congregation worked actively with that Convention. Sessions of the Convention convened mostly in Colorado although membership included congregations and individuals from the four states of Colorado, Idaho, Utah, and Wyoming. The delegates traveled by car, train, and bus. They stayed in the homes of various host families and ate their meals either at the host churches or in the private homes.

Western States Missionary Baptist Convention

The local congregations and the association of Black Baptist churches joined with other churches and associations of Colorado and Wyoming to work together as the Western States Missionary Baptist Convention. As early as the middle 1950s, members of the Utah churches traveled regularly to participate in the Convention sessions. The sessions provided for spiritual education, the election of officers, and planning of regional and national work. Some of those traveling included sisters Jessie F. Crowder, Martha H. Graham, Rosa B. Rowell, Lula Henry; brothers Nelson Styles, Theodore Twiggs, Edward Miller; and Reverends W. H. Hicks, William I. Monroe, J. L. Conners, and Benjamin J. Washington. These were pastors and lay leaders of Calvary, New Zion, and New Pilgrim. There were, indeed, exciting times for the Utah Black congregations to learn and grow through fellowship and education.

Reverend B. J. Washington

Alberta Henry Education Foundation

A number of African American students completed high school and needed financial resources to attend college in the middle 1960s. In response to their need, a scholarship program was established in 1965 by the Women's Association of the Utah and Idaho Baptist Association. The Women's Association had elected Mrs. Alberta Henry of the New Hope Baptist Church as their president at the February 1960 Board Session. She received donations from several friends to begin the scholarship fund.

In February 1966, Mrs. Henry resigned from President of the Women's Association of the Utah and Idaho Baptist Association due to her illness. Subsequently, the Association discontinued the scholarship program. The students were again left without funds to complete their educational program goals.

The students met with Mrs. Henry about their needs and agreed to work hard in fund raising activities. As the number of students increased, the money challenges became more than the students could meet. The fund raising efforts continued and some of the students took out loans. Finally, the students concluded their efforts with a banquet at the Newhouse Hotel on July 2, 1967 with the New Hope Baptist Church choir providing the musical selections.

A feasibility study was completed by Attorney A. Wally Sandack. As a result, more formal efforts began to get the fund operating again. The first meeting was held at the home of Mrs. Virginia Hiatt of Church Women United to formalize a foundation and to select board members. The students named the foundation the "Alberta Henry Education Foundation." The Foundation received its not-profit status on December 6, 1967 and has continued to serve students until now.

Mrs. Henry became chairperson and Mr. Ben Roe was elected treasurer to guide the Alberta Henry Education Foundation to numerous successes. Over 200 students have received moral as well as financial assistance to attend the University of Utah, Weber University, Utah State University, Salt Lake Community College and others. Selected on the basis of need, ability commitment, and performance, the Foundation supported students who have been Black, white, Hispanic, and Native American.

The Reflector

In an effort to "recognize, acknowledge, encourage and inspire" those toiling in extraordinary ways in God's vineyard,

Sister Sarah Monroe, wife of Pastor Monroe, published a monthly magazine. The second issue included contributions of Earlene Hopkins and Johnnie M. Wynne. Each edition would highlight the work and participation of some particular member of the congregation.

One of the most memorable issues of *The Reflector* profiled Brother Lawrence C. Wynne, who quietly served as trustee, choir president, deacon, and treasurer. He continues to watch over and safeguard the congregation's budget and financial resources at Calvary Missionary Baptist Church.

A Church Built On Dimes

Serious economic problems continued to confront the Utah congregations although they were reaching out to other Utah communities and surrounding states. On one occasion during the middle 1950s, the Rickett's Mortuary refused to take a body into the Calvary Missionary Baptist Church at 679 East 300 South for a funeral because the floor was so rotten. Shortly, thereafter, the mortuary sent a donation check of $500.00 for the congregation to repair the floor. With that gift, Pastor William I. Monroe started a building fund campaign with dimes. Members of the congregation used dime gleaners to solicit funds toward a new facility. Others of the congregation worked hard to raise funds by selling dinners and deserts while others gave as best they could. Then, the church borrowed some $105,000.00 from Prudential Federal Savings and began construction where the parsonage had been at the southeast corner of 700 South and Park Street.

The building was completed without pews, baptismal pool, or air conditioning. The building opened for occupancy and the congregation marched proudly from the old, over crowded, and deteriorating building into its new, modern, more spacious facility. Dedication services were conducted on Sunday November 3, 1966

Reverend William I. Monroe

with Reverend Dr. M. C. Williams of New Hope Baptist Church in Denver preaching and Sister Mabel Griffen leading the music. The celebration theme was "A Dream Come True," which was certainly the case, the congregation and ministry having built an entire church on dimes.

Some time later, under the administration of Reverend Henry L. Hudson between 1971 and 1972, additional funds were raised to secure items that would make the building more comfortable. Brother Eddie Williams, Jr. installed the two air conditioning units during early summer of 1972.

Sister Sarah Monroe

Baptist Youngster Enters Jury Box

Not only was there concern about buildings and facilities, but the Black Baptist congregations were concerned about the full human being. Salt Lake County District Court redefined the term "taxpayer" and on January 6, 1970 the first group of twenty-three year old citizens filled the court jury box. The previous jury members were usually about 55 years old. One of those young jury members was James Jackson, an active member of the Calvary Missionary Baptist Church. This father of four, who worked at the University of Utah's Medical Center, said in expectation, "I like to know what's going on, too. It will be a new experience; I might enjoy it."[60] This community involvement brought the Utah practice more in line with the United States Constitution, which required juries to be a

Brother James Jackson

"broad cross section of the citizens in the community." This new jury opened another door of opportunity for Blacks and other people of color.

The Utah Travelers Gospel Singers

Music has always been a central part of the African American experiences, especially in the Black church worship setting. About 1966, a small group of men who had been members of two previous groups of singers which had sung since the 1950s, organized themselves into one gospel singing group called The Utah Travelers. The original travelers were Arnold L. Spearman as manager, Leon Spearman, Jim Glasper, Richard Nelson, and Babe Ruth Jones. For the most part, they represented various Baptist congregations from both the Salt Lake City and Ogden communities although headquartered at either New Pilgrim Baptist or Shiloh Baptist. Their goal and purpose was to sing the music they had grown up with to the glory of God.

For approximately 30 years, the Utah Travelers have continued performing as Utah's longest and most active Gospel ensemble. They sing in churches, at festivals, for civic and educational functions, and in concert. They have appeared at a majority of the congregations of Black Baptists in Utah and the surrounding area. They have also sung along with well-known recording groups such as the Williams Brothers, The Bolton Brothers, James Cleveland, and Shirley Caesar.

The Utah Travelers have been faithful in helping maintain these musical and cultural traditions. "They blend Blues, R & B and Jazz into contemporary and traditional Gospel music." [61] The moving music provided by the group provides "spiritual and uplifting entertainment for the whole family." Their repertoire consists of old spirituals, gospel quartet standards and contemporary gospel music including many of their own original compositions.[62]

In 1991, The Utah Travelers received the Utah Governor's Cultural Heritage Award as recognition of their dedication to continuing gospel music, their contribution to understanding Black culture and heritage, and the joy they have brought to many Utah audiences through their performance of gospel music.

The Utah Travelers

Just-A-Portion

During the 1990s, other singing groups have emerged from the Black Baptist churches. Brian Hesleph called together some of the best trained voices at the invitation of Reverend France A. Davis and organized the popular "Just-A-Portion." They have been in great demand for community events as well as church programs. They sung with recording artist Michael Bolton, the Alabama Five Blind Boys, and John P. Key. "Just-A-Portion" sang for the last time as a group at the Calvary Missionary Baptist Church and Sundance Ski Lodge on Sunday December 22, 1996 as other opportunities took priority.

New Generation of Gospel

After leaving The Utah Travelers, where he played the guitar, James Morris started the contemporary gospel group called "New Generation of Gospel." The group continues to be available to fulfill engagements with inspirational music as they have done in the past with The Gospel Music Workshop, Shirley Caesar, the Williams Brothers, and the Bolton Brothers.

Second Baptist Church of Ogden

In 1971, Reverend Joseph Speech left New Zion Baptist Church in Ogden and took with him fifteen members to the newly organized Second Baptist Church of Ogden. The congregation provided a Sunday Radio program for the area until Reverend Speech departed in 1972. During the later half of 1972, Reverend Cal Carter took over the leadership. A short time thereafter the congregation opened and operated a child care center. The center met the needs of many African-American families and was open for any others. In the words of Reverend Carter, "I held the congregation together until Reverend James L. Gates became pastor in 1973.[63] Reverend Gates commuted from Sandy to Ogden to lead the congregation until he was called to Bethel Baptist Church in Pocatello, Idaho.

Later, the Second Baptist congregation published the "Gospel Truth" newspaper and the new pastor, Reverend Willie F. Martin III "provided piano lessons at no charge to anyone willing to learn."[64] With this congregation, Ogden provided two congregations to serve the spiritual needs of the Black Baptist community. Although organized in Salt Lake City, Revelation Baptist Church moved from Salt Lake City to Layton and on to Ogden. Under the leadership of Reverend Willie F. Martin III, the Revelation Baptist Church united with Calvary Southern Baptist Church of Ogden.

The Davis Brothers Team

After Reverend Speech departed Ogden and his nephew Reverend Henry L. Hudson prepared to leave Salt Lake City, two new faces moved in to fill the vacuum. Nearing the end of the summer of 1972, the arrival of Reverend Willie Davis from a small congregation in Wyoming to lead the New Zion Baptist congregation and Reverend France A. Davis from the University

Rev. Henry Hudson

of California at Berkeley/Oakland as A teaching Fellow and graduate student at the University of Utah signaled major changes for Utah's Black Baptist and community at large. These two ministers with the same last name, proclaiming themselves "brothers," began working as an inseparable team in 1973. They shared a common southern upbringing and spiritual heritage. Both understood the role of the Black Baptist Church to be about worship and daily living, making a difference in the community. For the next eight years, they served their respective congregations, led the Utah-Idaho Baptist Association of Churches, guided many other area efforts.

These two pastors led delegations to regional meetings held in such places as Denver and Colorado Springs, purchased and helped to drive newly secured fifteen passenger vans marked with church names and addresses to the National Baptist Congress of Christian Education, National Baptist Midwinter Board meetings mostly in Hot Springs, Arkansas, and to National Baptist Convention USA, Inc. sessions. For the first time large numbers of delegates from the Black Baptist Churches of Utah attended these national meetings. Among delegates

Rev. D. A. Washington

attending were youth, adults, and first-timer Deacon Walter Allen. Deacon Allen became so involved that he was soon destined to not only lead the Utah and Intermountain General Baptist Association Laymen's Movement but to become a major regional as well as national voice for the work at home and abroad. He was ofttimes introduced as "Mr. Utah" among his laymen peers. The team separated in 1980 as Reverend Willie Davis accepted the role of pastor at Second Baptist Church in Las Vegas, Nevada. Subsequently, he rebuilt that building into one of the finest multi-million dollar church facilities in that city. He said of his time in Utah, "Those were great times when we worked together, and were the best of friends."[65] Reverend France A. Davis remained in Utah at Calvary Missionary Baptist Church. He said of his ministry there, "They asked me in 1973 to fill in as pastor until they could find one. Now, here we are more than twenty-two years later and I am still filling in."[66]

In April 1996, the team shared with each other as Reverend France A. Davis preached the revival at Victory Baptist Church in Las Vegas. Then, in October 1996, they worked together when Reverend Willie Davis returned to preach Loyalty Week at New Zion Baptist Church in Ogden.

National Baptist Congress

With the educational level of Black Baptists increasing, the need for better trained church members caused the Utah congregations to seek courses of study. Various members of the Utah congregations participated in the training provided by the National Baptist Congress of Christian Education meeting in many locations across the USA. They completed courses of study and received certifications to teach certain courses such as "Sunday School Superintendent," "Old Testament," "New Testament," and "How We Got Our Bible." Several pastors and lay members received certifications to serve as deans and instructors of local and state congresses. As a result, the local association sponsored training courses for members of the congregations in the Intermountain area.

Presently, there are, for the first time in the history of Utah Black Baptists, five individuals from Utah working in leadership positions in the National Baptist Congress of Christian Education. Sister Dula Brock and Sister Shirley Brown are division coordinators. Brother Edward Miller is an afternoon discussion group leader. Brother Curley Jones serves as a board member of the National Baptist Congress of Christian Education. He also makes arrangements for delegate housing of not only his own congregation but for any others who request assistance. Pastor France A. Davis taught "Old Testament" until 1995. In 1995, he accepted the appointment as Special Assistant to The Dean, a position to which he has been assigned for 1997 as well. This participation on the national level brings more positive exposure to the work of Black Baptist in Utah.

Chapter 5
Light That Cannot Be Hidden

The work of Black Baptists in Utah makes life a bit more exciting for those who live within reach. The Gospel According to Saint Matthew 5:14-16 reminds us that people do not light a lamp to hid it under a bowl. Rather, they put it on a lampstand, hold it high, so that all who see it may enjoy its light. Black Baptists in Utah shine the light of stability and good deeds so that the Heavenly Father is praised.

Long Term Pastorates

Among the most long term pastorates in Utah have been that of Reverend Charles Spencer, Reverend William I. Monroe, and Reverend France A. Davis of Calvary Missionary Baptist Church; Reverend Benjamin J. Washington, Reverend L. K. Curry, and Reverend Willie Davis, all of Wall Avenue Baptist Church later renamed New Zion Baptist Church; and Reverend Ira L. Martin of Shiloh Baptist Church. Two major characteristics seem to be common contributors with those who served longest. Each found ways of working as team members with the church members and most had wives who, while loving the people, did not demand the spotlight. Currently, the most long term pastor in the history of any Utah congregation of Black Baptists has been Reverend France A. Davis who has served at Calvary Missionary Baptist Church since 1974, and continues to serve there today.

Property Taxation

Until 1974, the property and facilities of the Calvary Missionary Baptist Church and other independent, small congregations were being taxed by Salt Lake County taxing officials. When it was discovered that other, large church organizations received exemptions from this taxation burden, the Calvary Missionary Baptist Church, under the leadership of Reverend Davis, and the Trinity AME Church, led by Reverend Alvin Larkin, petitioned the commissioners to stop this unfair practice and refund monies already collected. Neither pastor received any sympathetic response to letters and phone calls, over a six-month time period. So they invited their respective congregations to join them at a public meeting with the officials. The press was present. The commissioners responded promptly to refund the taxes paid and discontinue further taxation of church facilities.

Utah Opportunities Industrialization Center

To assist the community with job training and placement, Mrs. Alberta Henry, clerk of New Hope Missionary Baptist Church, invited the Opportunities Industrialization Centers of America (OIC/A) to establish an affiliate in Salt Lake City for Utah. In 1974, a diverse Board of Directors was put together, funds were secured, and the Utah Opportunities Industrialization Center (UOIC) opened for business. The goals of this community based manpower training program were to provide "feeder" and skill training for individuals on welfare or with dead-end jobs, and to place then on jobs with upward mobility.

The Board of Directors elected Reverend France A. Davis, pastor of Calvary Missionary Baptist Church, to serve as chairman of the volunteer Board. He travelled to Philadelphia to received comprehensive Board training from the OIC/A Training Academy, in developing policy, overseeing executive staff, directing fiscal matters, and participating in fund raising activities.

The founder and chairman of OIC/A, Dr. Leon H. Sullivan (former pastor of Zion Baptist Church in Philadelphia, Pennsylvania) acknowledged the significance of UOIC by offering Reverend Davis as a candidate to serve on the National Executive Board (NEB) of OIC/A. Reverend Davis served faithfully and knowledgeably on both the national and local boards. Subsequently, he was elected secretary of the NEB, a position which he continues to hold at the time of this writing.

Unfortunately, funding and partnerships dried up for UOIC and, in September 1996, the Board voted to suspend all services and training for the foreseeable future. After obligations of the old organization are liquidated, perhaps a more focused, stronger, and reorganized OIC will emerge to help meet the future job training needs of Utah.

Ministerial Training

By July 1977, all except two of the churches had called new ministers. For the most part, this new group had little or no formal ministerial education and very limited pastoral experience. This was not surprising given the Black Baptists emphasis on "The Call" more than formal training and that the new pastors were relatively new in ministry. However, the congregational make-up was far more highly educated than in the 1940s and 1950s. The demands for ministry required better training and more experience.

With the help of Dr. Horace McMullen, through the Dayspring Program at Westminster College, and Reverend France A. Davis of Calvary Missionary Baptist Church, a $10,000.00 grant was secured to "train Black clergy." Basic courses including English, social studies, and speech as well as special courses were designed and taught on the Westminster College campus and at Calvary Missionary Baptist Church.

Experienced guest preachers, writers, and teachers were brought in to conduct workshops and seminars, including Dr. Gardner C. Taylor, Dr. Harry Wright, Dr. James C. Cone, Dr. James Reese, Dr. Clyde Miller and Dr. Henry Mitchell. These special guests spent three or four days conducting small group workshops with the Black ministers and preaching to the congregations in the evening.

In addition, Dr. C. E. Autrey had retired from his seminary teaching position and become the pastor of University Southern Baptist Church. He secured authorization to operate an extension of Golden Gate

Revelation Baptist Church

Theological Seminary and taught a variety of courses between the fall of 1979 and the spring of 1981. Black Baptist pastors enrolled and soon outnumbered the other students attending the classes.

These two efforts assisted pastors such as Reverends Isaac P. Brantley, France A. Davis, Theodore P. Fields, Lafayette Moseley, and Grover C. Walker to achieve much needed additional ministerial credentials and preparation. They provided strong learning experiences and intellectual exchanges. Black Baptists congregations reaped the benefits of better prepared ministers. All, except Reverend France A. Davis, have moved away from Utah to other fields of ministry: Reverend Lafayette Moseley to Las Vegas, Nevada; Reverend Theodore P. Fields to Union City, California; Reverend Grover C. Walker to McAllister, Oklahoma; and Reverend Isaac P. Brantley to Gainsville, Florida.

Intermountain General Baptist Association

The Black Baptist Churches of Utah and Idaho invited the Western States Missionary Baptist Convention to hold its 1975 annual session at Calvary Missionary Baptist Church in Salt Lake City. Pastors Willie Davis and France A. Davis were persuasive spokesmen for the effort. The delegates agreed to come and after much preparation the session convened. Many of those attending from Colorado arrived but complained about the housing and food expenses. In previous years, the delegates from smaller states went to Colorado without any assistance from the convention. When the session was cut short, the Utah-Idaho Association felt slighted and withdrew from the convention. The Utah-Idaho Association considered other relationship options, including association with Nevada or going into the National Baptist Convention USA, Inc., directly as a general Baptist association.

Ultimately, at the May 8, 1982 board meeting, the Association decided to join with other congregations from Idaho and Wyoming as a general Baptist association. That is, the Association would represent directly to the National Baptist Convention without going through a state convention. The investigation of other possibilities proved unsatisfactory. Dr. Mamie Oliver, wife of Pastor H. Lincoln Oliver and musician for the Boise St. Paul Baptist Church, suggested that the official name become "The Intermountain General Baptist Association of Churches, Incorporated (The IGBA)."[67] By 1991, the IGBA consisted of eleven congregations: Bethel Baptist of Pocatello, Idaho, Calvary Missionary Baptist of Salt Lake City, Utah, New Hope Baptist of Rock Springs, Wyoming, New Pilgrim Baptist of Salt Lake City, Utah, New Zion Baptist of Ogden, Utah, Revelation Baptist of Salt Lake City, Utah, Second Baptist of Ogden, Utah, Shiloh Baptist of Salt Lake City, Utah, Solid Rock Baptist of Salt Lake City, Utah, St. Paul Baptist of Boise, Idaho, and True Vine Baptist of Layton, Utah.

National Conventions Dual Alignment

Calvary Missionary Baptist, Wall Avenue Baptist-later New Zion Baptist, and Revelation Baptist have been, at times, dually aligned with National Baptist Convention USA, Inc. and the American Baptist Churches. Similarly, New Pilgrim Baptist, Shiloh Baptist, Second Baptist and New Hope have been, at times, dually aligned with the Southern Baptist Convention and National Baptist Convention USA, Inc. When congregations would not agree to become members of certain national conventions, pastors ofttimes joined as individuals. Two major issues seem to have led to dual affiliations. On the one hand, the National Baptist Convention USA, Inc. offers strong fellowship, educational training, and missionary cooperation. On the other hand, the American Baptist Convention and the Southern Baptist Convention provide extensive educational opportunity and fringe benefits for ministers. Within the last 12 years, the National Baptist Convention USA, Inc. has emphasized the later concerns. None of the national conventions operate with ecclesiastical authority over local congregations. Thus, with local congregations having voluntary relationships with national conventions, a majority of Black Baptists Churches in Utah hold membership in more than one body.

True Vine Baptist Church of Davis County

A large number of African-Americans moved into and lived in Davis County, on and around the Hill Air Force Base during the middle 1970s. Others enrolled into the Weber Basin and Clearfield Job Corps Centers. Among them, Reverend Grover C. Walker transferred into the area from Oklahoma to work in electronics. He united with the New Zion Baptist Church in Ogden. Living and working in Davis County, he soon discovered that no place of worship existed for Blacks in the county. After conducting the jail ministry for New Zion Baptist and commuting to pastor the Bethel Baptist in Pocatello, he returned to Clearfield and organized the True Vine Baptist Church in September 1978. He led the congregation with strong convictions that "Without faith, it is impossible to please God."(Hebrew 11:16)

After a short stay in a trailer court, the congregation rented a building across the street from Clearfield Job Corps Center. Later, they bought a building on Rainbow Drive. The Reverend Walker served faithfully until he felt the call to return to his home state of Oklahoma to restart the congregation where he grew up.

In August 1993, Reverend Jerome Council left his role as associate minister of Calvary Missionary Baptist Church and became the second pastor of True Vine Baptist Church in Layton, Utah. Almost immediately the congregation began a search for a new facility. They located a church building being vacated by the Kaysville Bible Church and, on Christmas day of 1994, became the first congregation of Black Baptists in Kaysville, Utah. This new facility was secured in time to host the August 1995 annual session of the Intermountain General Baptist Association. The director of Public Relations from the Sunday School Publishing Board, Dr. Brenda J. Holland, shared with the area churches during that session as the first National Baptist Convention, USA, Inc. official to visit the new True Vine Baptist Church facility.

Four locations of True Vine Baptist Church

IGBA Scholarship Fund

While some of the local congregations, including Calvary Missionary Baptist Church and Second Baptist Church, were providing academic scholarship assistance to their member students toward higher education, the Intermountain General Baptist Association instituted her own scholarship fund in August 1986. The Reverend France A. Davis became chairman of the fund. From funds donated by local congregations, Association auxiliaries, and from special fund raising, one scholarship is made available each year to each of the member congregations. Upon recommendation of the local congregation, the applicant would prepare and present orally as well as in writing a thematic message on an assigned topic at the annual session of the Association.

A total of eighteen students has received scholarship award checks from $200.00 to $1000.00 for each of the ten years of operation. The first of those students was Lloyd Cotton who has completed his preparation for full time ministry. He received support on an ongoing basis during his schooling. Other recipients of the Intermountain General Baptist Association scholarship have included Physhant Swenson, Evelyn Ashley, LaTangie Jones, Ja'Nelle Dixon, Kesha Houston, Greta Brown, Sean Thompson, Angela Wilson, Phillip White, Hanisya Massey, Michael Swenson, Khari Hawkins, Grace Davis, Scott Green, Patricia Otiede, Jacquette' Beard, and Anthony Carpenter. Reverend Isaac P. Brantley clarified our goal as he served as Association moderator: "...the task before us is great and it is clear: 'SAVE OUR CHILDREN.'"[68]

Dr. Martin Luther King, Jr. Holiday

To provide community organizing and support for a Martin Luther King, Jr. Holiday bill being sponsored in the 1986 session of the Utah Legislature by Senator Terry Williams, Reverend France A. Davis was asked by the Salt Lake Branch NAACP to chair a special committee. The primary task before that committee was one of educating the public as well as legislators. Through debate after debate, a major breakthrough resulted from a Take 2 television debate between Reverend Davis and Utah Representative Robert Sykes. The debate turned out to be a major educational session showing that Dr. King had spoken at the University of Utah, that his civil rights work was inclusive, and that the holiday would have a zero state budget fiscal note. At the conclusion of the half hour Sunday night program, Representative Sykes asked, "What can I do to make sure this legislation passes?" and signed on to become sponsor of the bill in the Utah House of Representatives.

In addition, Mrs. Coretta Scott King, widow of the late Dr. King, visited the area and spoke to the joint Senate and House on February 6, 1986. Members of the Black Baptist Churches in Utah were an integral part of the process and the resulting passage of a House Bill establishing the "Third Monday in January as Human Rights/ Martin Luther King, Jr. Day" in Utah.

Several years later, the community decided to request that a street be named for Dr. Martin Luther King, Jr. in Salt Lake City. The city was seeking to host the winter Olympic games and proclaiming to be open to the world. The Martin Luther King, Jr/ Human Rights Commission, with Reverend France Davis as a member, approached both the city and the state about renaming 600 South. It was the main access into downtown and had several critical sites including Trinity AME Church, Mignon Richmond Park, Trolley Square, Central City Community Center, and the Law and Justice Center. To designate this street Dr. Martin Luther King, Jr. Blvd. would signal those entering Salt Lake City that we are an open, accepting and inclusive community.

Like the passage of the Martin Luther King, Jr. Holiday Bill, this street designation debate required a good deal of education. Some opposition was racially motivated and resulted in hate mail and even name calling. After much negotiation, the proposal was approved and endorsed with the new sign cost to be raised by the community. New signs were prepared and hung.

Mignon Richmond Park

During the same year, the Salt Lake Branch NAACP, Trinity AME Church and the Calvary Missionary Baptist Church joined with others to get a park named for the first Black woman to graduate from Utah State University. Mrs. Mignon Barker Richmond had spent much of her life living directly behind where this new park would be located. She had worked tirelessly as a leader of the Calvary Missionary Baptist Church and as a community organizer. Mayor Palmer DePaulis and the Salt Lake City Council agreed to the name as proposed. The Reverend Davis, then, led the committee in raising funds to have made and installed a commemorative stone. The park was dedicated June 19, 1986 at 600 South between 400 East and 500 East.[69] It continues to provide space for special cultural gatherings such as Juneteenth and other recreational activities.

New Congregations By Division

Upon the death of the founding pastor, Reverend Ira L. Martin, of the Shiloh Baptist Church, Reverend Lafayette Moseley was installed August 10, 1980. When Reverend Moseley ran into trouble at Shiloh Baptist Church, he resigned in 1985 and organized Revelation Baptist Church on June 22, 1986. The new church moved into a small building at 601 South 900 West in Salt Lake City. Calvary Missionary Baptist Church donated hymn books and the first pulpit stand. The New Pilgrim Baptist Church donated hymn books, also. Both congregations lent chairs to Revelation Baptist. From the humble location on 900 West, Reverend Moseley moved the church next door to Jackson Elementary School.

Rev. Ira L. Martin and family

Shiloh Baptist Chruch

In 1988, Reverend Reginald B. Clinton became pastor and shortly thereafter moved the congregation from Salt Lake City to Layton, Utah. He left the area when reassigned by the U.S. Air Force. Subsequently, Reverend Willie F. Martin III became the pastor in 1990 and moved the congregation to Ogden. Then, the Revelation Baptist Congregation, needing a more permanent place to meet, united with the Calvary Southern Baptist Church of Ogden and took on the name of Calvary Baptist Church of Ogden. It was a natural match, as the former needed space and the latter needed members and leadership.

Following the departure of Reverend Moseley, the Reverend Herbert J. Lilly served the Shiloh Baptist congregation from 1987 until conflict arouse and the church doors were locked in 1989. He left, the church continued, and two new congregations were soon organized. Some members who left organized the Solid Rock Baptist Church under the leadership of Deacon Earnest Nixon in 1989, and they invited Reverend Walter Evans to become their pastor. Later, Pastor Lilly called together other followers and started the New Life Baptist Church of Taylorsville in 1992. Eventually, the Solid Rock Baptist Church and the Shiloh Baptist Church became one in 1992 under the name of Unity Baptist Church as led by Pastor Evans. The name Shiloh Baptist Church was dropped and the members became active participants in the new Unity Baptist Church. Some of the Solid Rock members refused to join the effort to unite two congregations and again the deacon Earnest Nixon started the New Solid Rock Baptist Church in 1992.

Calvary Tower Housing

When property west of the Calvary Missionary Baptist Church building to the corner of 700 South and 500 East became available, the church purchased it for approximately $200,000.00. Three duplexes and one house on the property soon proved to be more than the church thought it needed for expansion or could financially maintain. The church formed the non-profit Calvary Tower Housing, Inc. in 1986 and the United States Department of HUD was approached about a 202-government loan to build low-income elderly and physically handicapped housing units. The application to construct 30 one-bedroom units of housing was approved on July 10, 1986 with a loan amount of $1,008,100. A ground breaking ceremony was held and 30 units were constructed next door to the church building and opened for occupancy at a cost of more than 1.2 million dollars. Operating under a separate housing corporation and managed by Danville Development Inc., Sister Mary Green, a long-term member of the Calvary Missionary Baptist Church,

Calvary Baptist Church – 1995

became the third manager of the complex in October 1995.

From time to time, the Calvary Tower Housing residents complain about the Calvary Missionary Baptist Church members use of the adjoining parking lot which the Salt Lake City planning commission intended to be shared. The positive result of the project is that it provides housing for families who need it, and that housing is located next door to the church. These growth pains of the congregation and the commitment to human service cause problems but are preferred to the alternative.

Far West Regional Laymen's Workshop

Reverend France Davis

Feeling the need to touch and influence more Black men, and in its effort to promote more cooperation, the National Baptist Convention Laymen organized and began holding regional workshops on the state level. Historically, men have been less visible in our churches than are the women. In 1992, the Intermountain General Baptist Association hosted the fifth annual three-day meeting in Salt Lake City, Utah. Delegates of senior and junior laymen auxiliaries and conventions attended the April 10-12, 1992 session from Arizona, California, Nevada, Oregon, and Washington as well as Idaho, Utah, and Wyoming. What a time of excitement and fulfillment!

Brother Walter Allen, as president of the local laymen, dreamed of, prayed for, and worked hard toward the day when the meeting would come to our area. The seed was planted and began to germinate at the National Baptist Convention in Dallas, Texas, during the September 1988 session. The IGBA approved the invitation in its August 1989 session and the workshop agreed to come three years later. (Many of the national officials referred to Brother Allen as "Mr. Utah" because of his untiring commitment and almost singular representation of the area for years. On numerous occasions, when the local churches and association failed to come up with specific representation fees, Brother Allen paid them out of his own pocket rather than allow us not to be represented at all.) Brother Larry Houston as vice president, Brother Curley Jones as secretary, and Brother Lester Arney assisted and did much of the leg-work. Unfortunately, Brother Allen died not long afterwards, in July 1992, but with the assurance that his work was done.

As we approach April 1997, the workshop plans to return to Salt Lake City. The organizing and planning are moving full speed ahead, with Brother O. D. Lester from the True Vine Baptist Church as president and Brother Larry Houston of Calvary Missionary Baptist Church as committee chairman.

President of National Baptist Convention USA, Inc.

In 1993, the National Baptist Convention USA, Inc. came to a crossroads for many of the pastors and members. Five candidates surfaced for the office of president. Dr. Henry J. Lyons, who was serving as one of the vice presidents, contacted Reverend France Davis about coming to the intermountain area to share his vision. He was invited and came as the guest speaker for the One Hundred One Anniversary celebration of Calvary Missionary Baptist Church on November 14, 1993. He preached with power a sermon on "Unspoken Power" from Matthew 28:19-20. He met with pastors and sought the support of delegates from the area. With our support and under the banner of "Raising A Standard," he won the election in September 1994, by more than 500 votes, at the convention convened in New Orleans.

Subsequently, Dr. Lyons invited Reverend Davis to participate as a state president board member representing the IGBA and to serve as Special Assistant to the Dean of the Congress of Christian Education. Both of those responsibilities provide broader exposure and influence for the Black Baptist Churches in the intermountain states of Idaho, Utah, and Wyoming.

Reverend France A. Davis gave the following charge to the vice presidents of the National Baptist Convention USA, Inc during installation services on January 18, 1995 in Nashville, Tennessee:

> To President Henry J. Lyons, all officers and delegates to this board session of the National Baptist Convention USA, Inc.
>
> I am privileged to extend this charge on behalf of the

committee to those of you selected to serve as vice presidents. Will each of you please stand?

Having been selected to serve this august body is no small matter. Is it your intentions to accept the awesome responsibilities and to perform the duties entrusted to you?

Will you give of the best of your service?

Vice Presidents Response: We are committed to serving faithfully as Vice Presidents of this the National Baptist Convention USA, Inc.

Therefore, I charge you to be faithful servants, to perform the tasks assigned to you, to be available as needed to assist the President, and to act appropriately in word as well as deed. I charge you to preside fairly, to administer firmly, to watch over those entrusted to you care with love. Moderate decently and in order. Work together in a spirit of cooperation. May all you do promote the welfare of the Convention, the Church, the spread if the gospel of Jesus Christ, and be to the Glory of God.

AMEN![70]

14th Foreign Mission Preaching Team

In October 1995, Dr. William J. Harvey, III extended an invitation to Pastor France A. Davis to participate in the 14th Preaching Team of the National Baptist Convention USA, Inc. Foreign Mission Board. The Calvary Missionary Baptist Congregation agreed to release Pastor Davis for the month of February 1996, and to underwrite the estimated $3500.00 cost of the trip to southern Africa. The dream came true for Pastor Davis when he, along with Dr. Harvey and eleven other ministers, traveled to South Africa, Lesotho, Swaziland, Zambia, and Malawi for 24 days. The team visited various National Baptist schools, medical

14th Preaching Team

facilities, the 1000 acre farm, churches and preaching points in urban and bush settings. The need for more support and participation in foreign missions efforts became more real to each of the team members. As a result, the preaching team members were convinced to do more for foreign missions, not to take the privileges they enjoy for granted, and to stop complaining so much. They are determined to do their best and let their lights shine.

Although an overwhelming majority of the people in southern Africa live in extreme poverty, they seem to have discovered the secret of meaningful living. Like the Apostle Paul, they demonstrated "...For I have learned, in whatsoever state I am, therewith to be content." (Philippians 4:11b) They were overjoyed and excited that "the Black preachers with hair and skin like theirs from America" had come. Perhaps the greatest display of their excitement came when they had opportunity to give in worship and share gifts with their guest. They literally danced around when the time came to give their offerings.

Reverend Davis preached in urban as well as bush areas. Some facilities had no roofs, others had straw roofs, and still others had roofs that leaked badly. His sermon topics included "Building A House Dedicated To God" (Psalm 127), "The Need Of The Master" (John 4:4), "Wisdom Is Given" (James 1:4), and "Hope: An Anchor For The Soul" (Hebrews 6:19). He, also, gave the charge to Pastor Ray Dlemini who was installed at the mission church in Swaziland of February 14, 1996:

> "The best source I know for any charge to a new pastor is The Holy Bible. Let me start by charging you according to Romans 12:1-2: "I beseech you therefore brethren, by the mercies of God, that you present your bodies a living sacrifice, holy, acceptable unto God, which is your reasonable service."
>
> I charge you further according to I Timothy 4:16: "Watch your life and doctrine closely. Persevere in them, because if you do, you will save both yourself and your hearers."
>
> I charge you further with II Timothy 2:15-16: "Study to shew thyself approved unto God a workman that needeth not to be ashamed rightly dividing the word of truth. But shun profane and vain babbling for they will increase unto more ungodliness."
>
> Furthermore, I charge you from Titus 2:1: "...Speak thou the things which become sound doctrine."
>
> Then, I charge you from II Timothy 4:2: "Preach the Word, be instant in season, out of season; reprove, rebuke, exhort with all long suffering and doctrine."
>
> Finally, be the best you can be and then sing to the Lord, "Have Thine Own Way, Lord. Have Thine Own

Way. Thou Art The Potter. I Am The Clay. Mold Me
And Make Me After Thy Will, While I Am Waiting
Yielded And Still."
In short, PREPARE YOURSELF FULL.
PRAY YOURSELF HOT.
PREACH YOURSELF EMPTY."

The most effective sermons were basic and story oriented.
The people came to hear the Team gladly and over 200 committed
their lives to Christ during the tour. Worship music was without
instruments as we are accustomed to. The people kept time with
homemade guitars, hand-held pillows, and dinner bells. Their
harmony exceeded any I could remember. Each member of the
14th Preaching Team to Southern Africa wrote a trip response
which was published in the March/April 1996 issue of *Mission
Herald*. Reverend Davis said of the trip, "The experience will
never be matched or forgotten."

During the September 1996 meeting of the National Baptist
Convention USA, Inc. in Orlando, Florida, the February 1996
14th Preaching Team members were honored at the Foreign
Mission Banquet. Reverend Manuel Scott, Sr., Executive
Secretary of Evangelism for the National Baptist Convention,
USA, Inc. delivered an inspirational message on John 3:16
entitled, "The Two Pillars On Which Missions and Evangelism
Rest Are The Uniqueness and The Universality of Jesus Christ."
Reverend France Davis, Willene Davis, Melinda Humbert,
Doriena Lee, and Sylvia Morris were the five members of the
Utah Black Baptists delegation to participate.

There is no higher tribute to pay to Dr. Harvey than to call
him "Mr. Foreign Missions." He commented on his goal for the
14th Preaching Team as he gave his report to the National Baptist
Convention, "A knowledgeable people is a supporting people."
That remains a great description of the people being served and
those serving to accomplishing the work of National Baptist
Foreign Missions.

Western Regional Youth Conference

As the IGBA continued to reach out for fellowship, Sister Dula Brock took several young people to the National Baptist Western Regional Youth Conference meeting in other states. When she extended an invitation for the conference to come to Utah, Dr. Benecia Toms accepted the proposal and preparation began for the April 25-27, 1996 session. Several major hotels contracted to provide sleeping rooms, in spite of some problems with the booking agency. Abravanel Symphony Hall provided a rare opportunity to showcase the opening musical presented by the Angel Choir, Mass Choir, African-American Dance Troupe, and African Drummers. Merilyn Hesleph, director of the Intermountain General Baptist Association's Mass Host Choir, said of the music and dance participants, "I feel you have to keep kids busy or they'll find something to do that you don't want them to do."[71] More than adequate classroom, workshop, and general session meeting space was arranged in the newly renovated Salt Palace Convention Center, whose board chairman is Bernette Murphy, an active member of Calvary Missionary Baptist Church. Children ages two through eight met at Calvary Missionary Baptist Church for Bible Studies, crafts, and music while older delegates held their sessions at the Salt Palace. Some 2000 to 2500 delegates came including Dr. Cynthia Ray, the president of the National Baptist Convention Women's Department. Erica Houston of Salt Lake City's Calvary Missionary Baptist Church and a high school artist, did the art work which designed the conference T-shirts and program booklet.

Shaneka Daniels at the 1996 Youth Conference

For three days, the Salt Lake City African-American population swelled by nearly fifty percent. Some 2500 Black Baptists young people and their adult supervisors spent three day attending sessions at our convention center and church facilities. The Department of Christian Education taught classes on such topics as "I'm Feeling Pressure," "I Have A Choice," "Where Will The Black Church Be In The 21st Century," "Youth Leaders for the 21st Century,," and "Essence of The Black Man." The excitement and success of the conference in Salt Lake City are evidenced by young African Americans from Utah, Idaho and Wyoming already talking about attending and participating in the 1997 conference to be held in Tulsa, Oklahoma.

In addition, Western Regional Youth Conference planners are inquiring about another time for the meeting to return to Salt Lake City. Eighteen year old college student and IGBA Youth President, Taedra Morris summed it up: "The conference was very successful. The Christian Education classes were well prepared and served the purpose of providing us with a better understanding..."[72] These were, indeed, times of unprecedented spiritual excitement and light shining among Utah's Black Baptists youth.

Summary

Just as doors in the larger community opened wider for Blacks in the larger community, they opened for Black Baptists in Utah during the fifth, sixth, and seventh decades. New facilities were built on shoestring budgets and congregations emerged as membership grew. Better trained ministers guided their flocks in spiritual and civic affairs. Voices of hope echoed from the Black Baptists Churches calling the attention of others to a sparkling light.

With Utah Black Baptists teaching and supervising in the National Baptist Congress of Christian Education, hosting the Laymen's Regional Workshop, sponsoring the Western Regional Youth Conference, serving as members of the board for both the convention and congress, Black Baptists of Utah were thrust into the limelight. Reverend France Davis received many accolades for his charge to the National Baptist Convention vice presidents. For the first time within her over one hundred years, Black Baptists of Utah are recognized and respected among the leaders of Baptists not only in Utah but in the United States as well.

Furthermore, participation in the Laymen's Foreign Mission working tour and the Foreign Mission Preaching Team to Southern Africa shows Utah Black Baptists taking their rightful place as leaders all over the world. To be one of thirteen to travel in the five countries for twenty-four days announces unusual high regard with which Black Baptists of Utah are seen.

Epilogue
Where Do We Go From Here?
Visions For The Future

Having been a bright light in the Helper, Kaysville, Layton, Mohrland, Ogden, Salt Lake City, Sunnyside, and indeed, all of the Utah community, the Black Baptist Churches are documented dates as far back as 1892. While many other institutions throughout the larger community have been restrictive and exclusive, these congregations have continued to provide a refuge from a hostile world. They are open and mixed or integrated, although they remain predominately African-American. In fact, both congregational members and others of this community find life a bit more liveable and survivable through their experiences in and with the various Black Baptist congregations. The Bible teaches and the congregations accept by faith the Biblical wisdom, "Where there is no vision, the people perish. ..."(Proverbs 29:18)

Preparing For The Future

In order to position themselves for what is ahead during the concluding 1990s and into the third millennium, planning and goal setting continue. For example, New Zion Baptist Church purchased buildings and ground in their immediate area for possible parking and maybe building expansion. New Pilgrim Baptist purchased and moved into a huge facility with more than adequate parking, classroom space, and recreational facilities. New Solid Rock Baptist Church and New Life Baptist Church, although meeting in community centers presently, are both looking for buildings as more permanent places of worship and ministry. Unity Baptist Church opened a child care center.

Calvary Missionary Baptist Church, New Pilgrim Baptist Church, and Unity Baptist Church each operate some sort of computer literacy program. In addition, Calvary sponsors a Saturday School Project and houses the African-American Dance Troupe with drummers under the direction of Rita Bankhead-Grayson. At the present time, Calvary Missionary Baptist Church has outgrown her worship seating capacity and parking space. The congregation is negotiating for land to buy and build another facility with needed classroom and recreational space.

Office Management Options

With the congregations growing, staffing has had to increase. Some of them continue to operate with one primary person, the pastor carrying out most of the tasks. Calvary Missionary Baptist Church has opted to include additional volunteers to answer the phones, hand out clothing and food items, and to provide individual counseling. For example, "The Listening Ear" is available to listen, share, and help clarify options anonymously and/or in person.

New Zion Baptist Church has hired clerical office staff and, for a while, paid a full-time minister of music to direct the music department for regular worship as well as special services. More and more of the pastors are considering options for giving up their secular jobs and becoming full time pastors. For example, one option is to have larger congregations contribute toward the operating cost and pastor's salary of those smaller in numbers. Or, perhaps with a commitment to full time ministry and living in the specific community, the pastor will develop the congregation so that it is self-supporting.

Vision for Calvary Missionary Baptist Church

The Calvary Missionary Baptist Church continues to provide leadership in the Black Baptist Churches and Association of Utah. Pastor France A. Davis served three different terms as moderator of the Association during his more than twenty-two years as pastor of Calvary. He has served as State Vice President to represent the Intermountain General Baptist Association at the National Baptist Convention USA, Inc.

According to Pastor Davis, the Calvary congregation will consist more and more of all sorts of people. She will be integrated racially, politically, and economically. Yet, she will protect and nurture a distinct awareness of the Black heritage and culture. The young will mix with the older and the middle age. The number of children will decrease while the percentage of elderly will increase. Parents will attend more because of the benefits they see for their children than because of any personal commitment. Whatever individual commitments are made will tend to be more and more short term in keeping with the microwave/information generation.

We envision ministries ahead of us that will include something to supplement public school education, substance abuse counseling, food for the hungry, housing for the elderly and physically handicapped, and recreation for any who wish. We will pay special attention to the growing numbers of elderly and retirees.

We are in process with a building fund to purchase land, build a new facility, and move. We plan to hold on to the Calvary Tower Housing units and build a sanctuary with adequate classrooms for a school coupled with recreational/all-purpose space to feed five hundred sitting down. Adequate parking space and seating will be secured. After raising most of the projected three million dollars, we hope to move in approximately two years.

We expect that Calvary will be very active in all facets of life as it affects the daily existence of our people. She will keep spiritual matters first and foremost, while doing everything possible to meet any needs where people hurt. In other words, Calvary Missionary Baptist Church will take serious the mission of saving souls while caring for the least, the lost, and the last. Her light will lighten the path for all the community. She will, indeed, be the Church caring about people, warm, alive and well.

Vision For New Life Baptist Church

Under the leadership of Reverend Herbert J. Lilly, the New Life Baptist Church operates out of the Taylorsville Community Center. The congregation works with the association, helps to train young ministers, and provides an alternative place of worship on the southern end of the Salt Lake valley. As the body of members grow, they are reaching out in more ways than one, while welcoming newcomers. With more church experience than most of our local pastors, Reverend Lilly was elected as president of the Interdenominational Minister's Conference and as one of the IGBA vice moderators.

The New Life Baptist Church plans to move forward with a major educational effort. According to Pastor H. J. Lilly, "the membership of my congregation for the next decade will be Black people, ethnic groups with historical backgrounds, saints of God filled with the Holy Ghost and whosoever will, let them come."

"The congregation will be involved in teaching ministry, preaching ministry, healing ministry, training ministry for leadership in the church and evangelism, and a food and caring ministry... All of these ministries are important for the growth of a strong church or a strong congregation. Therefore, the teaching ministry is designed to instruct people in the Word of God, the Holy Scriptures, The Bible, especially Matthew 28:18-20. The preaching ministry is also needed. For the Gospel must be preached to the lost that they might hear and be saved. God has appointed prophets to preach the Gospel, to preach good tidings...to every nation."(Isaiah 61:1, Luke 15:15-17)

Sister Bessie Lilly was elected as President of the Intermountain General Baptist Association Women's Department. She made every effort to provide good leadership and teaching for the women to move forward. She served faithfully for two years while assisting her husband with the New Life Baptist Church congregation and working during the day in the Granite School District.

Vision For New Pilgrim Baptist Church

New opportunities opened up for the New Pilgrim Baptist Church as Reverend George Glass became the pastor. He came in as a strong preacher with a commitment to teaching and education. During the annual session in August 1995, the IGBA elected Reverend Glass to serve as president of the IGBA Congress of Christian Education. At the August 10, 1996 Association business meeting, Reverend Glass was installed as moderator for 1996-1997.

Reverend George Glass, Jr. said that the New Pilgrim Baptist Church in the 21st century will include members in the current occupations as well as "computer science, education, law, political science, medicine, and management."

"The ministries of the congregation will deal with "substance abuse programs, gang awareness, various areas of counseling, evangelism, and Christian education. Substance abuse programs will be a must because of the projected number of drug and alcoholic abusers predicted for the 21st century. Gang awareness will be very important because of the increasing number of gangs emerging in our communities and the number of young people who feel that it's cool to have gang association and the adults who don't have a clue as to what to look for as signs of gang involvement. Different areas of counseling will be needed because of the rapid spread of AIDS which will result in the loss of lives for many families, and the increasing number of divorces that will separate others. Evangelism and Christian education will be important in order to remain a growing church, evangelism to bring in new members and Christian education to keep them."

"The church facilities will consist of a computer lab, a family life center, nursery, library, children's Sunday meeting room, adequate classrooms, office space, and day care."

"It is my belief that the future role of the church must be to minister to the needs of the whole man, not just the spiritual man, but the physical man as well. For I hear Jesus saying, "When I was hungry you didn't feed me, I was thirsty and you didn't give me to drink, I was naked and you didn't clothe me, I was sick and in prison and you didn't visit me." (Matthew 25:37-39)

Vision For New Solid Rock Baptist Church

When the New Solid Rock Baptist Church began holding worship services, Reverend James Wilson accepted the position as pastor. He continues to serve the congregation as they grow and search for a more appropriate place to worship. Pastor Wilson and youth minister Elwood Stewart joined the Intermountain General Baptist Association the week of August 6-10, 1996. According to Pastor Wilson, the future is bright and hopeful.

During the next decade, the New Solid Rock Baptist Church will be primarily Black in its make up, although the people living in the area are predominately Hispanic and Asian. In fact, the community consists of families from at least six ethnic groups. The goal of the congregation is to persuade and win many to the Baptist faith.

To accomplish the goal, outreach ministries will provide food and clothing for those which are destitute and in dire need of assistance. In addition, youth ministries will offer a big brother/big sister type relationship for the young people who do not have brothers or sisters, and who may be residing in single family households.

As the congregation presently rents space in a multipurpose community center, the primary need of facilities is a church building with ample room for an office, for Sunday School classes, a large kitchen for preparation and service of food, and plenty of room for storage (a food pantry). The office will need to be reasonable size to accommodate a growing congregation and to house a computer which will store information concerning the church, church history, and track advancement/growth.

In general terms, the New Solid Rock Baptist Church can see a future of growth. "Our vision as a church is to live an obedient Christian life, professing our faith in Christ, sharing the message within our travels that salvation is free through Jesus, the Christ. We hope to reach as many people as the Lord wills. We will constantly seek ways to enlighten people and to diligently work for the gospel's sake."[73] (Note: Reverend Wilson left New Solid Rock and organized Wings of Grace Baptist Church in November 1996.)

Vision For New Zion Baptist Church

In February 1995, the New Zion Baptist Church installed Reverend George Merritt as leader of their flock. He was appointed by Moderator France Davis to work as liaison between the National Baptist Convention USA, Inc. Statistician Reverend Willie Davis and the IGBA. The congregation hosted the August 6-10, 1996 Annual Session of the Intermountain General Baptist Association.

"Operating under the command from Jesus to bring the lost to Him, the New Zion Baptist Church anticipates the members during the next decade will consist of old and new faces, different races, all ages, and all economic and political backgrounds. The church hopes to reach the local community and grow the church through entire families coming into the realization of Jesus Christ as their Lord and Savior."

"In order to accommodate this growth, there will be programs for the youngest to the oldest. There is a plan to strengthen the children's and youth Bible-based ministries by adding a long overdue recreation facility and computer lab. To meet the needs of the young adults, young married and singles ministries will be formulated. Since some of the anticipated growth will involve the Hispanic families neighboring New Zion Baptist Church, a Spanish speaking ministry will be formed. The adult and senior citizens' ministries will include daytime Bible study, prayer meeting, and other activities."

"The church presently has space for a recreation facility and computer lab, both of which are on our list of top priorities. Also, an educational building is among our wishes. It is not beyond our scope to build again if we run out of space in our present sanctuary."

"The overall role to be carried out by the New Zion Baptist Church congregation in the future is to be about the Lord's mandate which is to spread the gospel throughout all nations. This will be accomplished first in the local community and will spread throughout the surrounding towns and the state of Utah. Then, in the national work, New Zion Baptist Church will be instrumental in presenting the gospel throughout all the world. New Zion Baptist Church strives to be 'just a place where people can come to Jesus, receive spiritual nurture, and carry out Jesus' commandments.'"
(Note: Reverend Merritt left New Zion at the end of 1996.)

Vision For Second Baptist Church

Reverend Charles Petty leads the Second Baptist Church in Ogden. He worked with Reverend Glass in the position of vice president of the Congress. The future looks brighter for this 150-family congregation which is being forced to move from the place where they have worshiped for 25 years so the city can build a park on the location.[74] During the spring of 1996, the city of Ogden proposed a park to include their 33rd Street location. Now, they are actively negotiating for funds and a place to relocate to.

Reverend Petty said of the congregation's future: "We see/ project our members in the next decade as being very diverse in ethnicity, with the majority of them coming from the poor to lower middle income class. We also anticipate that they will have very little background in Christianity."

"We see our ministries as primarily "Reaching" (both in and out), "Maturing" (providing Scriptural substance that will stabilize trust and increase faith), and "Mobilizing" (recycling and sending those disciples back into the market places to start this evangelistic process all over again)."

"We see the need for our facilities to be more teaching/caring oriented. In other words, more classrooms to deal with the proper size for effective learning; more space that's recreational and conducive for the projected influx of children and youth, and space that will provide Senior citizens and elderly fun/fellowships. We also need spaces for nurseries and child care (both during and after church times, as well as more parking spaces)."

"We see the need for every individual member to live their lives and teach with a sense of urgency, like never before, as though they could literally see Christ coming down the street for them with a demand for their/our stewardship. I see our Families, Homes, Churches, Land, and World directly depending upon what the churches/lights do to get us back on the right track!"[75]

Vision For True Vine Baptist Church

A son of Calvary Missionary Baptist Church moves the True Vine Baptist Church congregation forward. Reverend Jerome Council emphasizes Bible studies and prayer as essentials for Christian growth and development. He serves as first vice moderator of the IGBA.

During the next decade, the True Vine Baptist Church has much promise. According to Pastor Council, "the membership will continue to be predominately African-American. As no Anglos are presently members, the first ones will join the congregation within the near future. Due to Hill Air Force Base being the primary employer in the area, True Vine Baptist Church will attract families from that military facility."

"The congregation will impact the demographics of the community through three primary ministries. First, others will be invited to unite with the Church by "Street Witnessing." Second, the special needs of mobile, military families will be emphasized. Third, the congregation will conduct outreach ministries with visitations to local hospitals and nursing home facilities."

"Having recently moved into a new building with sanctuary, classrooms, and a small gym, the facilities of the congregation will be sufficient for a while. However, space will need to be allocated for a child care/day care center, for a Christian school to fill the gap from public schools, additional classroom space for the church school, and the sanctuary will need to be enlarged to accommodate the new families and membership growth."

"I visualize True Vine Baptist Church evangelizing military members and their families, as well as any other unsaved in the north Davis and Weber Counties with the Gospel of Jesus Christ. Our role is to help hurting, broken, unsaved souls regardless of race or economic background." With his spirit of humility, Pastor Council will provide a much needed Christian shepherd for the Kaysville area.

Vision For Unity Baptist Church

Having come to this area in the United States Air Force, Reverend Anthony Simmons was ordained and installed as pastor of the Unity Baptist Church. He delivered the keynote address at the April 26, 1996 Western Regional Youth Conference in Salt Lake City.

Reverend Simmons says of the vision for Unity Baptist Church during the next decade: "The members of the congregation will consist largely of those between the ages of 18 and 30, of whatever occupations and positions they hold. We expect the young children to step up and fill different roles as the congregation offers what they are looking for.

"The Lord has shown us that the majority of the people have the gift of exhortation and if we tailor our ministry to our gifts, we will be a church that gets involved with ministries that service those that are less fortunate than we, while not neglecting to minister to all peoples of all types.

"We have been blessed because we own our church building, yet we will have to expand in the future. We already have classrooms yet our nursery is taking up much space.

"Our overall vision is that adversity can be over come and that for spiritual growth, not numerical-study and prayer is the key.

The Conclusion of The Matter

Throughout 104 years of history, the Black Baptist Church in Utah has weathered many storms, yet continued to meet the needs of the community. From one congregation, she has grown to nine at the present time. She operates as a worship center and a natural gathering place for community involvement. While serving primarily spiritual needs, these congregations have taken the lead in civil rights, political issues, cultural development, and economic cooperation. The impact of Black Baptists on Utah remains to be measured by the untold changes in generation after generation.

Out of a rich heritage dating back to 1892 and with a sparkling vision for the next millennium, Black Baptists in Utah are alive and well. The roads of obstacles and hardships provided stepping stones into the future. Each challenge has been a summons to move on up a little higher and to cause every round to go higher and higher. Upon the foundations laid by our forefathers, we expect our offsprings to do better and greater things than we have done.

With dreams and visions, Black Baptist Churches in Utah are going somewhere. They will make a significant difference in the well-being of those whose lives are touched. In the midst of the darkness of worldly ways, the light of expectation will brighten the pathway. They promise to call each individual to responsibility and accountability so that those who come behind will stumble less and go further.

Endnotes

1 Beckworth, Life and Adventures, 185

2 Coleman, Ronald G. A History of Blacks in Utah, 1875-1910, Unpublished Dissertation, (Salt Lake City: University of Utah, March 1980), pp. 74-79.

3 (Utah and The Early Black Settlers, p. 7)

4 Gerlach, Larry, "Vengeance vs. The Law: The Lynching of Sam Joe Harvey in Salt Lake City."

5 Savage, W. Sherman. Blacks in the West. (Westport: Greenwood Press, 1976), p. 84.

6 Fitts, Leroy. A History Of Black Baptists (Nashville: Broadman Press, 1985), p. 74.

7 Polk's Salt Lake City Directory, 1890.

8 The Broad Ax, April 18, 1896.

9 The Broad Ax, November 20, 1897.

10 The Broad Ax, June 18, 1898.

11 Salt Lake Herald, February 15, 1902

12 Butte New Age, June 13, 1906

13 Salt Lake Herald, January 26, 1902

14 Salt Lake Herald, February 9, 1902

15 Salt Lake Herald, February 15, 1902

16 Salt Lake Herald, February 16, 1902

17 Salt Lake Herald, February 23, 1902; Butte New Age, July 4, 1902

18 Rangon, Byrdie L., Utah and The Early Black Pioneers, p. 25.

19 Polk's Salt Lake City Directory, 1903, p. 70

20 Polk's Salt Lake City Directory, 1904, p. 72

21 Polk's Salt Lake City Directory, 1911, p. 76

22 "Obituary of Alice Sexton Steward," The Salt Lake Tribune, December 11, 1944.

23 Pedersen, Rose Mary, "The Gregory's-They Cared About People of All Races, Creeds," Deseret News. November 30, 1976.

24 Salt Lake Tribune, March 27, 1913

25 Harlan and Smock, The Booker T. Washington Papers., 1975, p.152

26 The Western Light, May 30, 1914

27 Doris Steward Frye Interview, 3/31/84, Side 1, pp 3-4.

28 Mary Elizabeth Barker Smith Interview, February 22, 1983, S1-7.

29 Mortgage signed by Mrs. Lena Dallas, church clerk.)

30 Souvenir Brochure and Dedication Celebration, October 26, 1958.

31 Receipt January 9, 1968.

32 Agreement between the American Baptist Home Mission Society and the Utah Baptist State Convention, October 4, 1928.

33 Minute book of Utah Baptist State Convention Board of Managers, pp. 151, 167, 212, 219, 240, 340.

34 "Proceedings of the Sixth Annual Session, Utah, Idaho and Wyoming Baptists Association, August 16th, 17th, 18th, 1923.

35 Constitution and By-Laws, Article 2.

36 Constitution and By-Laws, Article 8, Section 3.

37 Constitution and By-Laws, Article 3, Section 1.

38 Proceedings of The Sixth Annual Session, August 1923.

39 Constitution and By-Laws, Article 9, Section 2.

40 Proceedings of the Sixth Annual Session, August 1923.

41 Wallace was a significant voice of the Harlem Renaissance. He is in fact considered as one of the pioneers of this significant juncture in American history when African American culture was in vogue. His novel, The Blacker The Berry The Sweeter The Juice, is considered one of the most important work of that period.

42 The Young Folks Dramatic Club program.

43 Pedersen, Rose Mary. "The Gregorys-They Cared About People Of All Races, Creeds," Deseret News. November 30, 1976, p. A-11.

44 Harmony Will Embrace Us All. Salt Lake City, 1995, pp. 8-9.

45 Calvary Baptist Church History, 1976, p. 5.

46 Calvary Baptist Church History 1899-1976, p. 6.

47 Souvenir Brochure and Dedication Celebration, October 26, 1958, p. 3.

48 Interview with Mrs. Anna Morris, May 2, 1996.

49 Interview with Mrs. Anna Davison Whitehorn Morris, May 15, 1996.

50 New Pilgrim Baptist Church History, 1973.

51 The Rocky Mountain Messenger, March, 1946, p. 3.

52 "Excerpts from the Moderator's Annual Address, Minutes of Rocky Mt. Association, July 12-14, 1944. pp. 7-8.

53 Minutes of Rocky Mt. Association, July 12-14, 1944.

54 The Rocky Mountain Messenger, March, 1946.

55 The Rocky Mountain Messenger, December 1945, p. 3.

56 The Rocky Mountain Messenger, March 1946, p 14.

57 Souvenir Brochure and Dedication Celebration Program, October 26, 1958, p. 3.

58 New Hope Missionary Baptist Church of Salt Lake City, Utah, History and Aim, 1968.

59 Letters from Dwight S. Dodson, July 8, 1954; William I. Monroe, August 5, 1954; and receipt September 1, 1954.

60 Deseret News, January 6, 1970, pp. B-1, B-12.

61 -, "Uplifting Tones of Utah Travelers To Be Heard," Eagle Newspapers, June 27, 1996, p. M9.

62 Unpublished History of The Utah Travelers, July 30, 1996.

63 Interview with Reverend Cal Carter, November 1, 1996.

64 A celebration of Twenty Years for Second Baptist Church, September 22, 1991, p. 2.

65 Introduction by Reverend Willie Davis at Victory Baptist Church in Las Vegas, May 18, 1996.

66 Thank remarks at 22nd Pastor's Anniversary, April 27, 1996.

67 Souvenir Program 74th Annual Session, August 6-10, 1991

68 Brindle, Reverend Isaac P., "Youth Department Proposal." February 10, 1990.

69 Letters and notes in Calvary Baptist Church files, 1985-86.

70 Davis, Reverend France A. "Charge to National Baptist Vice Presidents, Nashville, Tenn. January 18, 1995

71 Deseret News, "Metro", Saturday, April 27, 1996, p. B1.

72 Interview with Taedra Morris, May 23, 1996.

73 Survey completed by Pastor James Wilson, August 4, 1996.

74 Whaley, Monte. "Park Will Replace Ogden Neighborhood," The Salt Lake Tribune, June 10, 1996. pp. D-1, D-4.

75 Survey of "Future Vision Church Survey," by Reverend Charles Petty, July 17, 1996.

76 Edwards, Jane, "Mignon B. Richmond: Community Builder," The Salt Lake Tribune, February 19, 1995. p. J3.

77 Christianson, Joyce. "'Mother' DeBies Loves To Help Others," *Deseret News*, February 11, 1978, p. 4A.

78 Interview with Frederick DeBies, July 31, 1996.

79 Remarks made by Reverend France A. Davis during Eulogy of Mother Ella Louise DeBies, January 1985.

80 Interview with Mrs. Ella Louise DeBies, February 1974.

81 Oliver, David H., A Negro On Mormonism, U.S.A., 1963. p. 7.

82 Interview with Edward Miller, July 22, 1996.

83 Interview with Deacon Nelson Styles, September 9, 1996.

84 Interview with Edward Miller, July 26, 1996.

85 Interview with Edward Miller, July 26, 1996.

86 Interview with Edward Miller, August 5, 1996.

87 Interview with Edward Miller, August 5, 1996.

88 Interview with Mary West Rucker in Salt Lake City, August 16, 1996.

89 Interview with Mary West Rucker at Salt Lake City, August 16, 1996.

90 Interview with Mary West Rucker in Salt Lake City, August 16, 1996.

91 Interview with Ernest Nixon in Salt Lake City , August 16, 1996.

92 Interview with Ernest Nixon in Salt Lake City, August 16, 1996.

93 Interview with Clydies and Ray Finn, July 29, 1996.

94 "A Condensed Biography of Our Pastor: Benjamin Jefferson Washington," 1958.

95 Letter to the Members of the New Zion Baptist Church from Reverend B. J. Washington

96 Interview with Clydies and Ray Finn, July 29, 1996.

97 Interview with Clydies and Ray Finn, July 29, 1996.

98 Interview with Clydies and Ray Finn, July 29, 1996.

99 Theme of Souvenir Brochure and Dedication Celebration Program, October 26, 1958.

Appendix I

List of Black Baptist Churches in Utah

1. Calvary Missionary Baptist Church of Salt Lake City, Utah - 1892 Started as a house church by Sister Emma Jackson and became known as "The Baptist Prayer Band." Calvary Missionary Baptist Church is the mother church of Black Baptists in Utah.

2. Wall Avenue Baptist Church of Ogden, Utah - 1914 Moved under Reverend Benjamin J Washington 1956 and renamed by Sister Jimmie Lee Wilson to become New Zion Baptist Church.

3. Sunnyside Baptist Church of Carbon County, Utah - 1919 Continued for very short time.

4. First Baptist Church of Mohrland, Utah - 1922 Active in the Utah, Idaho, and Wyoming Baptists Association. Disbanded in 1927.

5. Pilgrim Baptist Church of Salt Lake City, Utah - 1922 Started as a split by Reverend George Hart(s) and members from Calvary Missionary Baptist Church due to pastor moral problems and the organizing of his organizing of the Utah, Idaho, and Wyoming Baptist Association.

6. New Hope Baptist Church of Salt Lake City, Utah - 1954 Started by the Reverend Jesse Killings and disbanded in 1977 after the Reverend Isaac P. Brantley resigned. Money from the property sale was divided between Calvary, Shiloh, New Pilgrim, and the Alberta Henry Educational Scholarship Fund.

7. Pilgrim Baptist Church of Helper, Utah - 1958 Led by Reverends George Harris, Ira L. Martin, Douglas A. Washington. Property was abandoned and later sold in the 1970s.

8. Shiloh Baptist Church of Salt Lake City, Utah - 1965 Organized as a Southern Baptist Mission by the Reverend Ira L. Martin in 1971. It was located first at 715 South West Temple, moved November 1965 to 800 South West Temple, Congregation combined with Solid Rock to become Unity Baptist in 1992. The name Shiloh Baptist Church was dropped.

9. Second Baptist Church of Ogden, Utah - September 1971. Started with members who left New Zion with Pastor Joseph Speech. Incorporated January 21, 1972.

10. True Vine Baptist Church of Clearfield, Utah - October 1977. Officially organized by Reverend Grover C. Walker September 1978. Moved into Ridgewood Estate Mobile Court Recreation Hall October 16, 1977. Rented first church building in Clearfield across from Job Corps Center at 160 East 1799 South August 12, 1979. Moved to 288 West Gordon Ave in Layton June 1986. Purchased building at 1323 North Gordon in Layton February 1987. Moved again under new pastor Jerome Council to 197 West 100 South in Kaysville on December 25, 1994.

11. Revelation Baptist Church of Salt Lake City, Utah - 1986 Started June 22 and opened for service July 6 by Reverend Lafayette Moseley upon his leaving Shiloh. Second Pastor Reginald B. Clinton moved church to Layton. Third pastor Willie F. Martin, III moved congregation to Ogden and later combined it with the Calvary Southern Baptist Church of Ogden. The name Revelation Baptist Church was dropped.

12. Solid Rock Baptist Church of Salt Lake City, Utah - 1989. Started by Deacon Earnest Nixon and members who left Shiloh Baptist due to conflict. Reverend Walter Evans became the first and only pastor.

13. Unity Baptist Church of Salt Lake City, Utah - 1992. Reverend

Walter Evans combined Shiloh Baptist and Solid Rock Baptist. Reverend Anthony Simmons served as Interim Pastor and was elected Pastor in 1994.

14. New Life Baptist Church of Taylorsville, Utah - 1992. Started by Reverend H. J. Lilly after he departed as pastor from Shiloh Baptist. Several members of Shiloh Baptist formed the core group of New Life Baptist Church.

15. New Solid Rock Baptist Church of Salt Lake City, Utah - 1992. Started by Deacon Earnest Nixon. Reverend James Wilson became pastor and remained until November 1996.

16. Wings of Grace Baptist Church of Layton, Utah - November 1996. Started by Reverend James Wilson.

Appendix II

Roster of Utah Black Baptists Pastors

Calvary Missionary Baptist Church

1898	Reverend A. E. Reynolds
1899-1900	Reverend D. Jones
1901-1904	Reverend James W. Washington
1904	Reverend Charles O. Boothe
1905-1906	Reverend Lee A. Brown
1907-1908	Reverend John H. Allen
1911	Reverend William A. Magett
1912-1914	Reverend Allen Newman
1914-1916	Reverend Manasseh H. Wilkerson
1916-1923	Reverend George W. Hart(s)
1924-1925	Reverend J. D. Wilson
1926	Reverend John M. Riddle
1927-1929	Reverend Mack Stovall
1931-1932	Reverend George Hooie
1932-1941	Reverend Charles Spencer
1941-1947	Reverend William A. Lucas
1948-1950	Reverend William L. Holloway
1950-1951	Reverend Andrew W. T. Chism
1951-1953	Reverend Lester L. Agent
1954-1967	Reverend William I. Monroe
1968-1970	Reverend John H. Johnson
1971-1973	Reverend Henry L. Hudson
1974-present	Reverend France A. Davis

First Baptist Church

1923-	Reverend M. H. Flemmings

New Hope Baptist Church, Salt Lake City

1954-1956	Reverend Jesse Killings
1956-1957	Reverend George Harris
1958-1965	Reverend Ira L. Martin
1965-1967	Reverend Aaron N. Conley
1968	Reverend F. D. Brown
1974	Reverend James L. Gates
1975-1978	Reverend Isaac P. Brantley

Pilgrim Baptist (New Pilgrim) Church

1923-1926	Reverend Walter J. Brannon
1926-1928	Reverend Walter T. Bartlett
1930	Reverend Edward W. Booker
1947-1952	Reverend Jesse Killings
1954-1959	Reverend Louis D. Williams
1959	Reverend Aaron N. Conley
1960	Reverend Elroy Day
1961	Reverend Burnett Lane
1962-1964	Reverend Douglas A. Washington
1971-1972	Reverend Morris Broden
1973-1977	Reverend M. J. Robinson
1977-1991	Reverend Theodore P. Fields
1992-1994	Reverend Clifton Wilkes
1994-present	Reverend George Glass Jr.

Wall Avenue (New Zion) Baptist Church

1917-1919	Reverend Alex J. Billingsly
1919-1920	Reverend Henry L. Marque
1920-1921	Reverend John W. Morris
1922-1923	Reverend Moses A. Eilonth
1924	Reverend Lemuel A. Garrison
	Also pastor of First Baptist
1924-1925	Reverend James L. Washington
1925-1927	Reverend James E. Moore
1927-1928	Reverend D. D. Banks
1930-1936	Reverend Lucious A. Platt
1937-1938	Reverend Israel Craft
1938	Reverend J. L. Jones
1939-1940	Reverend Paxton
1942-1948	Reverend Jesse L. Conner
1948-1951	Reverend J. L. Rollerson
1952-1962	Reverend Benjamin J. Washington
1963-1964	Reverend S. C. Miller
1965-1968	Reverend Lacy K. Curry
1969	Reverend Olice E. Piper
1970	Reverend Leodis Winston Watkins
1971	Reverend Joseph S. Speech
1972-1978	Reverend Willie Davis
1979-1983	Reverend N. Lawrence Liggins
1984-1986	Reverend Tyrone Seals
1987-1994	Reverend Isaac P. Brantley
1995-1996	Reverend George Merritt

Pilgrim Baptist Church of Helper

1958	Reverend George Harris
1960-1964	Reverend Ira L. Martin
1965-1970	Reverend Douglas A. Washington

Note: This congregation no longer operates and no records were located to provide accurate and certain dates.

Revelation Baptist Church

1986-1988	Reverend Lafayette Moseley
1988-1990	Reverend Reginald B. Clinton
1990-1994	Reverend Willie F. Martin III

Shiloh (Unity) Baptist Church

1965-78	Reverend Ira L. Martin
1980-1986	Reverend Lafayette Moseley
1988-1989	Reverend Herbert J. Lilly
1992-1994	Reverend Walter Evans
1995-present	Reverend Anthony Simmons

Second Baptist Church

1971-1972	Reverend Joseph Speech
1973-1974	Reverend Cal Carter
1974	Reverend James L. Gates
1975-1984	Reverend Willie F. Martin, III
1985-present	Reverend Charles Petty

True Vine Baptist Church

1977-1992	Reverend Grover C. Walker
1993-present	Reverend Jerome Council

Solid Rock Baptist Church
1989-1992   Reverend Walter Evans

New Life Baptist Church
1992-present   Reverend Herbert J. Lilly

New Solid Rock Baptist Church
1992-1996   Reverend James Wilson

Wings of Grace Baptist Church
1996-Present   Reverend James Wilson

Appendix III

Utah Para-Church Organizations

1. Utah State Baptist Convention
2. Utah, Idaho, and Wyoming Baptist Association - 1918
3. Western States Baptist Convention
4. Utah-Idaho Baptist Association
5. Evangelistic Hour on KWHO Radio - February 1974. Started by Reverend Douglas A. Washington to share Gospel music and inspirational messages.
6. Intermountain General Baptist Association of Churches, Inc. Involves congregations from the three states of Utah, Idaho, and Wyoming.
7. Rocky Mountain Baptist Association

Appendix IV

Future Vision Church Survey Form

1. Who will the members of your congregation be during the next decade?

2. What ministries will the congregation be involved in and why?

3. What facilities will the church need and have to meet the needs of the congregation and the community?

4. What is your overall vision of the role to be carried out by the congregation in the future?

Appendix V

These were years of growing excitement and progress for Black Baptists in Utah. Among other things, Mrs. Mignon B. Richmond, a member of Calvary Missionary Baptist Church, graduated from West High School in 1917. She went on to become the first African-American to earn a degree from Utah State University in 1921. She had been born on April 1, 1897, just five years after Calvary Missionary Baptist Church started, and became an active member of the congregation, where she served in various leadership roles until her death on March 11, 1984 at 87 years old. Her neighbor and fellow member of Calvary Missionary Baptist Church, Mrs. Elnora Jennings remembers: "She was really interested in young people, wanting them to make something out of themselves."[76] While she had no children of her own, Mrs. Richmond can be credited with helping everybody else to make a better place to rear their children.

Others identify Mrs. Richmond as a "good Christian woman" who served as Sunday School superintendent as well as chairman of the Calvary Trustee Board. She enjoyed Christian hymns such as "Trust and Obey" and "Count Your Many Blessings." These favorites inspired her faith and walk. In spite of her own experiences with the pressures of prejudice, she sought to prepare the way and build community for others through strong commitment and unwavering faith in God.

While still alive, numerous honors were given to her, and the tributes continue to be directed toward the memory of Mrs. Richmond. In 1986, a park directly behind her house was named "Mignon B. Richmond Park. In 1992, Utah State University designated a multi cultural students and scholarships society the

"Mignon B. Richmond Society." Nearly a full page news story was published about her on Sunday February 19, 1995 by the director of the YWCA, where Mrs. Richmond served as a volunteer between 1923 and 1972. During January 1996, the Centennial Commission honored several women including Mrs. Richmond. She was, indeed, a light in both the spiritual and educational vision for Black Baptists in Utah.

Ella Louise DeBies

The Black Baptist Church reaped great benefits when Mrs. Ella Louise DeBies settled in Utah in 1927 as a single parent after migrating from Ashland, Kentucky through Kansas and Missouri. She had been born just about one year before Calvary Missionary Baptist Church started on October 11, 1891. She had married Oscar Lawrence as a teenager but later divorced him. To their union was born a son Zelmar Lawrence who graduated from the University of Utah with a degree in Journalism in 1930. She said of her move to Salt Lake City, "Because I did not have a lot of schooling because my family moved a lot doing construction work, I wanted my son to have a good education, and he chose the University of Utah."[77] She joined the Calvary Baptist Church on September 17, 1927. Later, she met and married John Frederick DeBies in 1929 who came to the United States from a capital city of South America. They adopted and reared four year old Juanita and seven month old Frederick.

The Black Baptist Church, and Calvary Missionary Baptist Church in particular, would not have been the same without Sister DeBies who was affectionately known as "Mother DeBies." According to an interview with Brother Edward Miller, she and her two adopted children were three of the five people present at Calvary Missionary Baptist Church that first Sunday night he was in town during 1942. Her son Frederick recalls her church participation, "She was very active in Church...morning, afternoon, and evening. She was not wanting to be in charge or leader, but always wanted to be involved."[78] Yet, records indicate that Mother DeBies served in almost every leadership role that women could hold except that of an usher. For more than fifty years, she was a deaconess, a choir member, and a missionary society member. From 1973 until 1984, you could expect to see "Mother DeBies" almost everywhere you saw Pastor France Davis including the National Baptist Congress of Christian Education in 1980 at St. Louis, Missouri. Reverend Davis said, "I was young and inexperienced as a pastor, so I took her with me to keep the rumors and temptations that plague many a young minister from taking over. You might say she was a shield for me. Besides, she enjoyed going. When it was time to go, she was always ready."[79]

She described her schooling as a "leap and jump, from here to there. I went to a little red country school. It had one room with a monkey heater." Yet, the real secret to her well-spent life was her unwavering faith in God, her willingness to help others, her faithful attendance and participation in worship, her liberal giving, and her firm principles and beliefs. She said of them in the February 11, 1974 issue of *The Broadax* newspaper, "I'm just different, old fashioned and funny like that."[80]

Whenever services or programs were being held at Calvary Missionary Baptist Church, if no one gave her a ride, "Mother DeBies" would walk even after her 90th birthday. She served faithfully and gave liberally until her departure from this life on January 6, 1985. Her funeral was a grand home going celebration.

Attorney David H. Oliver

In 1931, a middle-aged yet energetic attorney, David H. Oliver passed the Utah State Bar and moved to Salt Lake City. He had previously graduated from the University of Nebraska in 1920 with an LLB Degree and was admitted to the Nebraska Bar in 1923. His opportunities to perform as a lawyer were very limited due to racial prejudice. Although trained to practice law, he took a dining car job and came to work in Ogden as a waiter for the Union Pacific Railroad.

Once in Salt Lake City, Attorney Oliver united with the Calvary Missionary Baptist Church by Christian Experience. He helped to fashion the constitution and bylaws which the congregation operates under. He described his experience in his book *A Negro On Mormonism*, "I was converted and baptized in the New Hope Baptist Church at Oakwood in 1909, have maintained membership in the Baptist denomination ever since, and am now a member of Calvary Missionary Baptist Church in Salt Lake City, Utah."[81]

Attorney Oliver served faithfully and actively as a member of the Calvary Missionary Baptist Church Trustee Board and as legal counsel. In business meeting, he served an unofficial parliamentarian helping to keep order within the framework of the church constitution and bylaws. Edward Miller served alongside him and said that the larger community thought highly of his legal expertise. "They would often say of Attorney Oliver, "His delivery maybe poor but he knows the law,. I hate to go up against him. He is the smartest lawyer I know."[82]

Howard and Marguerite Browne

By 1939, Carbonville, Utah was no place for Howard and Marguerite Browne to rear and bring up their children. So they left the coal mining community and moved to Salt Lake City. Although having some formal training in medicine, Mr. Browne worked as a Carbonville miner and later from Salt Lake City as a railroad man. He wanted out of that central Utah community where a Black man was lynched. He worked hard with his hands around the house and on the job. During his retirement years, he managed and maintained four rental housing units owned by the Calvary Missionary Baptist Church.

Mrs. Browne served in various church activities and would do anything to be helpful to her pastor. In spite of her many negative experiences with discrimination in the work place, she lived a philosophy of "Move over, I'm coming through." Her church activities included the superintendent of Sunday School, teacher of Sunday School, clerk and treasurer.

The Howard Browne family along with the Nelson Styles family were, during the most difficult financial years, the only tithers at Calvary Missionary Baptist Church. Ofttimes, the trustees had to wait until their money came in to pay the bills.

Deacon Nelson Styles

"In January 1942, I came to Utah to serve in the United States Army/Air Corp at Camp Kearns directly from the Savannah, Georgia Induction Center. Twenty-two years old, I served as a soldier for the duration of the World War II until 1946. My starting pay was just $21.00 per month but eventually increased to sergeants scale. It was not until sometime in 1948 that I first attended the Calvary Missionary Baptist Church under the leadership of Reverend W. L. Holloway. The small congregation was ofttimes divided over leadership and financial issues. Reverend Holloway moved to Denver in August 1950.

"The friction continued as Reverend A. W. T. Chism accepted the leadership in December 1950. Having served as Dean of Theology at Western Baptist Seminary in Kansas City, he saw the challenge for church growth in the area. His threats of disciplinary action against church members and his leadership style stalled both the church business and activities.

"After Reverend Chism departed in August 1951, the congregation invited Reverend L. R. Agent to be the pastor of Calvary in October 1951. He assigned Sister Phyllis Grayson and Sister Gladys Hesleph to organize and direct a Young Adult Choir. Members who had left began to return and Calvary hired

Sister Beverly Morgan as at $50.00 per month as the first secretary. Then, bad luck struck again. The congregation dismissed the trustees and audited the financial records. Both actions resulted in separate law suits and the congregation split. Reverend Agent resigned July 1953.

"In March 1954, Reverend William I. Monroe and his wife Sarah moved to Salt Lake City from Cheyenne, Wyoming. He started a drive to build a new church. He ordained me along with Brothers Willie Hesleph, Joseph Brown, Harding Jones, and James Etherly to be deacons. I was a soloist in the choir and doing lots of special work. Sister Ridge and Sister Hesleph did special work and gave me much encouragement. I did most funerals and sang at other churches such as New Pilgrim Baptist and New Zion Baptist.

"Reverend Monroe worked hard and completed the new church building at 532 East 700 South. He left feeling he had done all he could do. He could not take the church any further. What a legacy he left. He did not want his deacons smoking and used to say, "If God wants you to smoke, He would have put a smoke stack on your head." He taught us to be careful what we did and as leaders not to do certain things in front of people. He didn't want us going to Ogden and "Junie Flipping" or "Jolly Flopping." (Note: "Junie Flipping" and "Jolly Flopping" are terms used to describe the behavior of those out in the world having a good time and living it up.)

"One story he told that I still remember: 'There was a little boy who was so bad that his father decided to drive a nail into a tree every time he did something wrong. He kept getting worse until the tree was just about full of nails. Then the little boy decided to change and his father would pull a nail out of the tree for every good deed. Eventually, all the nails were removed but the boy was disturbed because the scares were still there.'

"For a very short time, Reverend John Henry Johnson led

the congregation from February 9, 1968 until 1971. He never did get too active with the deacons. He wanted new deacons every year, not ordained ones. He ran into lots of problems and the church asked him to leave.

"Determined to root out the problems, Reverend Henry Hudson accepted the challenge of getting the church members working. He stayed with the deacons and met with us all the time. He let us know what was expected, what "Thus saith the Lord." He insisted that we be real and genuine, together not fighting. He did not do much to reach out to the young people. Eventually, he surprised everybody when he decided to move on. He came that morning and preached, "If The People Won't Hear You, Shake The Dust Off and Move On." Sister Phyllis Grayson whispered to me, "I think he is getting ready to leave us." At the end of the service, he resigned and told the deacons that he had already moved, and that they should ask Reverend France A. Davis to carry on until they could find a pastor.

"Now, Calvary is at its peak especially with young people. Reverend France A. Davis came with new programs, new progress and everybody understanding and cooperating. He taught us to know what we are to do and to do what we are to do. When you can't do what you know you ought to do, nobody will have to ask you to step down. You will do it yourself. The right spirit exists now. Most of the other churches are seeing the light and following leadership. The right people are working with the right people. We just need to shed more light on the program and get more people involved with it.

"I was a delegate for four years in a row from the Calvary Missionary Baptist Church Baptist Training Union to the National Baptist Congress. I went to Buffalo, New York; Memphis, Tennessee; Birmingham, Alabama; and Denver, Colorado. I had one more year before I could have graduated and gotten a certificate. We used to fellowship under Reverend Monroe with First Baptist and Murray

120

Baptist. We held services yearly in the mountains and sometimes baptized in the Jordan River.[83]

Edward Miller

While working as a bell hop in Cleveland, Mississippi during 1942, Mr. Edward Miller caught a glimpse of a better opportunity. He waited on a man with Utah license plates and gave him his name and telephone number. Miller said, "If you ever need a good man in Salt Lake City, let me know." Shortly, thereafter, the manager of Fort Douglas Golf Club called and offered him a one way ticket and a job. He came to Salt Lake City and worked for several months, saving his money until he could send back for his family. He said, "I had a wife and two boys, I brought them to Salt Lake City so they could get an education 'cause I didn't want them to go through the hardship that I had. I wanted my boys to get a good education. Being here they could go all the way from kindergarten through college. So we settled here and we lived here every since.[84]

The first Sunday night he was in Salt Lake City, Miller took a cab to the Calvary Missionary Baptist Church at 679 East 300 South. He shocked and surprised the five people present, Reverend and Mrs. Lucas, Mrs. Ella Louise DeBies and her two children Frederick and Juanita. He united with the congregation two weeks later but his job with the Pullman Company kept him from attending very often. He performed nonessential work with the Pullman Company until World War II ended.

In order to have more time with his family and church, Miller quit the train job after the war and went to work for American Smelter Refining Company. "I started with a wheelbarrow, a shovel, and a push broom." After eighteen years of work in different day-pay positions, he went as the first Black man to go salary with the company. He worked as a supervisor until his retirement January 1, 1981.

"I remember while Albert Fritz was president and I was the

vice-president of the Salt Lake Branch NAACP, Nate King Cole came to perform at Lagoon in 1961 during Kennecott Copper Day. We contacted his people and made a noon appointment to meet with him. When we arrived, his assistant informed us that he was resting and that we should return at 4:00 P. M. At 4:00 P.M., the assistant brought word that Cole was meeting with the Lagoon management. An hour later, he sent word that he knew what we were up too and he could not meet with us because he was under contract. If he broke it he could be sued.

"For the next two years, the union president refused to let his members participate in any Lagoon Day saying, "We are all union men and if these boys (We were called boys then, not men.) can't go in, there won't be no Lagoon Day.

"Then in 1964, Fats Domino came to sing for the Lagoon Day. When he saw no Negroes on the dance floor the first night of his performance, he asked the restroom employees what the problem was. They included Blanche Hopkins and Ruby Taylor, two members of the Calvary Missionary Baptist Church. They explained that the swimming pool and the dance floor were off limits to us. He instructed them to get in touch with as many blacks as they could find and have them there for the next night. He said, "If they don't get admitted at 7:00 p.m., there won't be any music. My music is for all people." We showed up by the car load and Fats Domino told the management to let us in. Lagoon management was concerned about trouble starting. He explained to them, "The NAACP president is here and my people don't cause no trouble. There won't be no trouble, at least, not from our side." So, they let us in and that started the break up of segregation at Lagoon and with Kennecott.

Another time, Albert Fritz called me and said Westminster college had a scholarship they wanted to give to some upstanding Negro. We got Jerolyn Jackson to apply and then I took her with us to the Western States Missionary Baptist Convention in Denver.

She got both the Westminster and the Western States Missionary Baptist Convention scholarships.

Miller watched the Calvary Missionary Baptist Church grow from very few in attendance under Reverend Lucas to an influx of military related families under the younger and energetic Reverend Agent. He participated in the local church as well as the Utah-Idaho Baptist Association, the Western States Missionary Baptist Convention, and the National Baptist Convention, USA. Inc. Attending many of these meetings along with him was Mrs. Rosa Rowell, Mr. Nelson Styles, Mrs. Jessie Crowder, Mrs. Martha Graham and Reverend B. J. Washington and his wife. He was elected to the executive board of the Western States Convention for two years. Afterwards he concentrated on the Congress of Christian Education with Mr. Harvey McDaniels and Mrs. Jessie Crowder. Miller became vice president of the congress and served for five years with Reverend B. J. Washington as convention president and Mrs. Jessie Crowder as congress president. Then, he was elected to the position of Congress president for an additional five years. During the same time period, he served as trustee and superintendent of Sunday School at Calvary Missionary Baptist Church.

Miller remembers several very difficult times for Black Baptists in Utah. On one occasion, the congregations could neither pay the pastors salaries, the church rent or note, nor provide heating for their facilities. In fact, money was so tight at one time that when three members stopped paying, the church could not pay the monthly mortgage. He recalls a time when Calvary Missionary Baptist Church Member, Attorney David H. Oliver purchased a white house on 400 East at 700 South. "...at that time the LDS church owned the property. When they found out that they had sold it to a black man, at that time we were Negroes, they broke the contract and gave him his money back. The house was too good for a Negro to own that house."[85] Perhaps the worst of all experiences came when the NAACP organized one Friday night to boycott and picket at the Utah State Legislature. The ministers disagree and Saturday morning hand delivered a letter stating, "We are the Negro Ministerial Alliance and we want to inform you that the NAACP will be picketing at the state capitol on Monday afternoon. We are not in support of this picketing."[86] (The picketing did take place but the people were so disappointed in their leaders that they talked about removing them.)

Miller and Mignon Richmond worked with the larger community to help bring the job corps center to Clearfield, Utah. It was quite a struggle fueled by the fear of many that some 500 blacks would be infused into the area from Mississippi and Alabama. After some time, the center was established and continues to provide basic education and skilled training for many young people from across the USA.

In short, Edward Miller came to Salt Lake City more than fifty years ago. He emerged as a leader in the Calvary Missionary Baptist Church, the Association of Baptist Churches, the Western States Missionary Baptist Convention, the National Baptist Convention, on his job in copper mining, and in the local civic and fraternal organizations. Although well beyond the four score years promised in Psalm 90, he continues to help look out for the welfare of Black Baptists in Utah. He reports of the progress we have made, "The Lord sure has blessed us and I am a witness."[87]

Jesse and Thelma Tucker

"In July 1943, I came to Ogden, Utah from Arkansas. My wife Thelma didn't joined me until that September. I first worked for construction and later for both the OUR and D and Southern Pacific Railroads, and the Navy base. We joined the Wall Avenue Baptist Church under Reverend Rollerson in 1946. He didn't stay too long, but he seemed to be awfully nice.

"Reverend B. J. Washington came next. He did lots of good

church building. One thing about him, he worked himself right along side of everybody else. We just paid him the salary we agreed on and nothing else. He was a good leader and got along so well with everybody. When he came from Cheyenne, he told the church that we don't have any money but we are going to build the Church. People all around town helped with donations. He went to the lumber company and told the man, "We don't have any money." He left and when he returned, the man told him to go to building and whenever he needed anything to show up himself, not to send anybody. He was everybody's favorite pastor. Obie Blackmore paid the $100.00 toward digging the basement. It took us until 1956 to finish and march in. Reverend Washington helped to build New Pilgrim, too.

"Reverend L. K. Curry came after Reverend Washington left. He was a good man but the church just would not do too much. They would not cooperate, so he got another church and left for Chicago.

"The greatest contribution of Wall Avenue Baptist Church, now known as New Zion Baptist Church, was the building and the people sticking together. The people raised money with some of them mortgaging their houses.

Mary West Rucker

On September 5, 1944, Mrs. Mary West Rucker came to join her husband D. B. Rucker who was stationed as part of the United States army at Camp Kearns. As he had made no arrangements for her to have decent housing, she returned to Louisiana where she stayed until November 1944. Upon her return to the Salt Lake City, she moved into a basement apartment at 176 East 700 South owned by a Mrs. Jefferson. She became a member of the Calvary Missionary Baptist Church on Easter Sunday morning 1946 under the leadership of Reverend Lucas. "I liked him. He was an awfully nice minister. He was quite a serious person, and a big man."

Mrs. Rucker worked with the youth of the congregation

including the George Henry, Willie Hesleph, and Reeves Smith boys. She taught them many things including how to prepare the table and bless it for a banquet. "We had a tuna fish, potato chip, and punch banquet."[88] She remembers, "I encouraged them that if there was anything right to do and they wanted to do it, to do it. And one of them went off over seas and another went out acting."[89] On one occasion I was teaching them that "if you are going to drink, you take the drink but don't let the drink take you,' and the pastor came in and told me that nobody could do that. I didn't know what he was trying to tell me until I found out he had a big drinking problem.

According to Mrs. Rucker, Reverend William I Monroe was the most memorable minister prior to Reverend France Davis. Reverend Monroe had a great sense of humor. "He could make you chuckle about something and then turn around and knock you down with the Gospel... He taught me not to be so quick to give up because you will never know what the end was going to be... He could bring out things to be enjoyable. I really liked him as an older man carrying the gospel just as I like Reverend Davis as a young man carrying the gospel with such a long way yet to go."[90]

Following Reverend Monroe came Reverend Henry Johnson who was originally from Louisiana. He was very special, an honest, down to earth person. His attitude was, "Accept me as I am and don't try to change me." He was always wanting to get things done. His wife seemed to be the cause of many of his problems here at Calvary. He finally got in trouble with the church about his use of some credit card. The trustees borrowed money to pay him off so he would leave.

Now, we have Reverend France Davis who does not know what his potential is. He has no idea where he will one day go or how many or what churches he will get to pastor. He can go anywhere and do so many things. "Mrs. Lula Henry has so much

126

faith in him, I hope nothing ever happens to disappoint her. Calvary has come such a long way."

Deacon George Anderson

"I am eighty years old and I came to Utah on January 20, 1946. Reverend J. L. Rollerson was the pastor at Wall Avenue Baptist Church in Ogden. He lived in a little three-room parsonage, a shot-gun house. The deacons back then were Ira Martin, Hinton, Lewis, Joseph Graham, Higden, and Crowder. Reverend Rollerson made Della C. Lee, Walter Allen, and me deacons. I was singing in the choir for a while under Sister Louise Cooper as director. Deborah Walker, sister of Sister Finn, was church clerk. Rev. A. C. Done was president of the Western Baptist States Convention.

"After Reverend Rollerson died one Sunday after he preached, Reverend Garcia and Reverend Conner from Pocatello tried to get the Wall Avenue Baptist Church. They didn't make it. Then, Reverend Benjamin J. Washington came with two conditions: we would buy a new parsonage and agree to build a new church. We started building real soon. A man named Anderson sold us the land for the church and it had a house on it for a parsonage. I think he sold it to us for about $900.00. I know it left us with just $43.00 in the church."

We went to work on building the church. We dug an eight feet by eight foot hole, hauling the dirt by wheel barrel. We were just pushing and carrying, pushing and carrying. We weren't making no money, but the people had their hearts in it. Reverend Washington always said, "The people could give all the money we need at one time, but they won't. You have to have a three o'clock program and sometimes even an evening service to get all the money you need."

"He asked for $100.00 from all the officers. I had an old forty-nine Chevrolet that I had turned in on a Pontiac. I had

$300.00 more to pay on it but I needed to pay $200.00 to the church for my wife and me. So, I went to Mr. Fisher of Fisher-Hess Pontiac Company. He told me to go in the office and pay the clerk the $300.00 and come on back out through his office and he would give me the $200.00. I tell you, if you do right, God will bless you.

Ira Martin and Marion Carter put all the wiring in the building. We had different clubs who helped to raise money and to keep the people busy working. When the man with the crane didn't come, we borrowed a long block-n-tackle from the shop. We used it with a jit-pole to raise the rafters. We found an old boiler and Marion Carter put it in the basement so we could have heat. It made a lot of noise, always popping."

Everybody was asked to go down to Ford Finance and sign for a loan. The lowest amount was $300.00. I signed and from then on I was paying out $40.00 a month more than I was drawing on the job. I was doing some shade-tree machining and had more money than ever. The Lord will bless you if you give.

"When we got ready to go to the Western States Missionary Baptist Convention, Reverend Washington would load up his car and then mine. They would give me $12.00 for the trip. So you see how little money there was. Reverend Washington ran into so trouble and left. He wrote back and asked the church to give him two or three years leave. The church would not go along. The church called Reverend S. C. Miller from Sanford, Texas but he couldn't make it.

Then, Reverend Lacy K. Curry came from a little church in California. He said we were going to pay the church off. Everybody wanted to know where we would get the money from. We raised $12000.00 in just three months. Reverend Curry was a real business man. He was a good man but he was better suited for that big church in Chicago.

He was followed by Reverend O. E. Piper of Wichita Falls. He just stayed for about a year and moved on to Dallas, Texas to take another church. Reverend L. W. Watkins came for about nine months and left. Reverend Joseph Speech moved in and stayed until he was discharged. He had already organized Second Baptist Church when the church voted him out. He asked the deacons if he could make an announcement at the business meeting. He stood up and said, "All for the pastor meet me at 301 33rd Street Sunday Morning at 11:00 a.m. The Millers, Maxwells, Pearlie Sanders, Martha Graham, the Beasley's, Queen Darby, and others went with him. Some of them didn't last long and came back.

The church was without a pastor for a while. When the Western States Missionary Baptist Convention held it annual session at New Zion, everybody seemed to have been assigned a place to stay except a young fellow from Wyoming. I told him he could stay at my house for two nights. I told him he wasn't nothing but a boy. Later when the church asked me about him, he came and stayed for six years. They never gave him a raise up off of that $60.00 a month. He could fill a house but he found another church and moved to Las Vegas. We had another struggle.

Brother McGowan went to Texarkana and brought Reverend N. L. Liggens name in. He was a good preacher. His trouble was that the church gave him too much power. He didn't want to have to come to the church for everything. He wanted the authority to just go ahead and do without coming back to the church. The church let him do it. Now, he could get people together. Then he left.

The next preacher was Reverend Tyrone Seals. He came for his trial sermon on a day when the Grand Lodge of Sorrow was there. That was the wrong day to have him come. He unbuckled that Sunday and the people went wild. After he came, several people had daughters who came around every day. He asked some of the people to come and be around there, but he never asked me. So, when trouble started, he had to leave, too.

Reverend Isaac P. Brantley had been around, up in Wyoming

and other places. He came to back to New Zion where he had preached his first sermon and been licensed. He had one of the best wives that I had known. After a while, I stepped down and told them to put one of the younger fellows in my place. I served twenty-eight years as chairman of the deacons and Reverend Brantley gave me an appreciation plaque in 1990. I was getting so that I had to get away from the deacons. The many different medicines I was on had me so I could hardly walk to that mailbox. He went on until he decided to leave.

"Now, this man they have now... I don't know what's going on now, cause I don't let nobody tell me nothing about nobody 'cause they always tell you the bad but never nothing good."

Deacon Ernest Nixon

One of the most long term deacons of a Black Baptist Church in Utah is Deacon Ernest Nixon. Born on December 17, 1922, he moved from Detroit, Michigan to take a job at Hill Air Force Base, Utah in May 1945. He continued that job until the victory over Japan in August 1945, about three months. From there, he got a job with Denver and Rio Grande Railroad along with Howard Browne and others. He united with the Pilgrim Baptist Church at 300 South in 1952 under the leadership of Reverend Jesse Killings as the church was being rebuilt after the fire.

About three years later, the Reverend Louis D. Williams led the congregational move to a new location. Reverend Benjamin J. Washington was general contractor for the building of New Pilgrim Baptist Church facility. Reverend Williams worked longer and had better relationship than any of the pastors remembered. "He was best known for his work with youth and helping churches to grow. He used the term "church building." Maybe that's why he moved around so much."[91]

Deacon Nixon remained a member at New Pilgrim Baptist Church until 1975 when he and several others went to Shiloh Baptist

Church. He served there for about twelve years and left with Leon Spearman, Mary Shaw and family, James Glasper and family, Mrs. Albert Daniels, and Thomas Sykes and family to organize the Solid Rock Baptist Church. While the attempt to reunite the Shiloh Baptist congregation and the Solid Rock congregation as Unity Baptist Church was somewhat successful, Deacon Nixon led others in starting the New Solid Rock Baptist Church in 1993.

Some of the most dedicated church workers sharing with Deacon Nixon at the various locations included Joe Bates, Emma Brown, Annie Adams, Eddie Adams, and Mae Nixon. According to Deacon Nixon, "The Black Baptist Churches worked with a cooperative spirit, especially when Reverends Benjamin J. Washington, William I. Monroe, Louis D. Williams demonstrated a spirit of togetherness. They operated what you call a School of Religion. They were the major points of contact and fellowship for Blacks in Utah. I would love to see a stronger influence on our community, especially to help our Black boys in the way they are going, to give more direction. Of course, the churches can only do what the churches do. They can offer but that's all. You don't know whether the people are saved or not but you can bear witness that they went through the water."[92]

Clydies and Ray Finn

For $37.00, Mrs. Clydies Wesley Finn joined her sister in moving from Stamps, Arkansas to Ogden, Utah in January 1946. She became a member of the Wall Avenue Baptist Church in March 1946 under the leadership of Reverend Jessie L. Conner from Okmulgee, Oklahoma. As a single parent, she met and married Mr. Ray Finn who was also a single parent. Together, they reared their children as active members of the Wall Avenue Baptist Church. Although Reverend Conner preached and conducted Bible Study while his wife played the piano, attendance was sparse. Some of those attending were Deacon and Sister Dellie

C. Lee, Deacon and Sister Joseph Graham, Deacon and Sister Clarence Hampton, Deacon and Sister George Anderson, Mrs. Jessie Crowder, Mrs. Vada Bea Myles, Mrs. Annie Huff, Mrs. Pearlie Sanders, and Mrs. L. A. Platt.

Mr. and Mrs. Finn remember that Reverend J. L. Rollerson of Denver, Colorado was called to Wall Avenue Baptist Church in the summer of 1948 and stayed until he died on December 5, 1951. "That Sunday morning, he preached, went out to the house behind the church, laid down, and didn't get up anymore."[93] He was discovered dead by family and friends. The undertaker refused to pick up his body until a doctor came out and pronounced him dead.

The big change occurred in Wall Avenue Baptist Church when they extended a call to Reverend Benjamin J. Washington. He accepted the call and moved from Second Baptist Church in Cheyenne, Wyoming on April 3, 1952 with the stipulation that "the people would help him to build a new church." Reverend Washington's acceptance prayer was: "Oh God! Thou hast assigned to me a great task. Make me a better man to do a bigger job! AMEN!"[94] Like the Biblical prophet Nehemiah, Reverend Washington came with his mind made up to work, and work he did. The building process started promptly with the purchase of a lot in February 1954. Ground breaking ceremonies took place on May 16, 1954. Members of the church arranged to borrow so much money from the Ford Finance company toward the building. The Finns borrowed $450.00 the first time but went back later to get more. Whatever money was available each Sunday was applied to the building. Reverend Washington did the building with his own hands and the help of the men and community volunteers. The ladies brought food and drink. The facility was dedicated debt-free as the words of Reverend Washington were remembered: "Our AIM is to Dedicate this "House" also, to the Service and Glory of God, DEBT-FREE October 26, of this year. Remembering always: "We can if we Will. We will if we care.""[95]

Reverend Washington experienced family problems which continued to fester despite the attempts by Reverend M. K. Curry of Central Baptist Church in Denver to help resolve them. While making plans to leave for a while, he asked the deacons if he could return when he got himself together. Having been told emphatically, "No," he left ten years after his arrival during the spring explaining, "I don't think I will be back." Mrs. Finn says lovingly, "He was really a good man. He lived here with us for a while and he always treated me the same no matter whether Ray was here or not."[96] Many remember Reverend Washington as that "good man" who was hardworking and liberal.

Reverend Lacy K. Curry accepted the New Zion Baptist Church in 1968 while he was still a seminary student. He traveled back and forth to school during the week. Unlike Reverend Washington, he insisted that the congregation pay him what they had agreed upon. The Finns remember, "He would tell the people what he thought...and he would want to do something, but the people would not let him."[97] Reverend Curry became known as a doer who was always on time, who cared and shared with everybody.

The Finns have served at New Zion Baptist Church under the leadership of seven additional pastors including Reverend Willie Davis. Mrs. Finn says, "I worked in Wall Avenue Baptist Church, now New Zion Baptist Church, for fifty years in many roles including Mission president, Ushers president, Deaconess president, and district association Ushers president several times. In fact, I was the first president of the association's ushers."[98] Mr. Finn works as an usher and a deacon. With long term hard workers like Mrs. Clydies and Mr. Ray Finn, New Zion Baptist Church lives up to her reputation as "The Church Built By Faith."[99]

Edna Martin Washington

"I remember that Florence Shepherd had a brother who lived in Helper, Utah. They had a little church on the hill about 1950. They would have ministers come on Saturday, stay all day, have worship services on Sunday morning, and leave to Salt Lake City in the afternoon. Reverend Ira L. Martin went down for about three and one-half years. Then, he returned to Ogden to work with Reverend B. J. Washington as his associate minister.

"Some time in 1958, Reverend Martin was called to serve as pastor of New Hope Baptist Church in Salt Lake City. He led the Utah-Idaho District Association during 1963-64 as its moderator while Sister Alberta Henry of New Hope Baptist Church was District President of the Women's Department. He served faithfully until 1965.

"Then, on May 9, 1965 Reverend Martin founded and organized the Shiloh Southern Baptist Mission which was first in a one room house located at 715 South West Temple. There were thirteen charter members. Before too long, the congregation moved to 800 South West Temple in November 1965. As the body began to grow, an eight-member choir was formed. A year later the congregation moved again to 634 South 400 East and continued growing and expanding through 1973.

"The city wanted that property to building housing and the church once again began the process of moving. On April 13, 1975, we marched into the building at 1170 West 1000 North. The congregation worked hard as the Lord blessed. On July 10, 1977, Brother Jerry Barnes preached his first sermon entitled, "An Undoubted Faith" and was licensed by the congregation.

"Reverend Ira L. Martin continued the fight in spite of his health limitations. The congregation was saddened by the death of their leader/pastor on December 28, 1978. These were hard emotional times as the shepherd had been called home and the sheep were left to find their own way. During the next year's time, leadership was provided to the congregation by Reverends Lafayette Moseley, Isaac P. Brantley, and Caige Featherson.

"On August 10, 1980, Reverend Lafayette Moseley was installed as the second pastor for Shiloh Baptist Church. He set a new goal of paying off the church mortgage by the beginning of 1984. Indeed, the entire community was invited to participate in the Mortgage Burning Ceremony on December 23, 1983. The press release stated: "For there is another man with a dream-A dream to build within the church and to fulfill the needs of the community and with the faith of this small congregation and the guidance of this man, Shiloh moves forward.'

Bibliography

"A Celebration of 20 Years for Second Baptist Church." Ogden: Second Baptist Church. September 22, 1996.

"Baptist Youngster Enter Jury Box." Salt Lake City: Deseret News, January 6, 1970.

Alter, J. Cecil. *Early Utah Journalism.* Westport, Conn.: Greenwood Press, reprinted, 1969.

Beckworth, James P. *Life and Adventures.* Minneapolis: Ross and Haines, 1965.

Brantley, Reverend Isaac P. *"Youth Department Proposal,"* Ogden: February 10, 1990.

Calvary Missionary Baptist Church Papers. Salt Lake City: Calvary Baptist Church. 1985-1996.

Carter, Kate B., comp. *The Story of the Negro Pioneer.* Salt Lake City: Daughters of Utah Pioneers, 1965.

Christianson, Joyce. *"Mother DeBies Loves To Help Others,"* Deseret News. Salt Lake City. February 11, 1978.

Church History Committee, comp. Calvary Missionary Baptist Church, 1899-1976. Salt Lake City: Calvary Baptist Church, 1977.

Coleman, Ronald G. *A History of Blacks in Utah,* 1825-1910. Ph.D. Dissertation. Salt Lake City: University of Utah, 1980.

Constitution and ByLaws. Utah, Idaho, and Wyoming Baptists Association. Ogden: Wall Avenue Baptist Church, August 20-24, 1918.

Davis, Reverend France A. *"Charge to Pastor Ray Dlemini at National Baptist Church in Swaziland, Africa."* February 14, 1996.

• *"Closing Remarks at 22nd Pastor's Anniversary."* Salt Lake City: Calvary Baptist Church. April 27, 1996.

• *"Eulogy of Mother Ella Louise DeBies."* Salt Lake City: Calvary Baptist Church. January 1985.

Dodson, Dwight S. *"Letter to Calvary Baptist Church."* Ogden: American Baptist Archives. July 8, 1954.

Edwards, Jane. *"Mignon B. Richmond: Community Builder."* Salt Lake City: The Salt Lake Tribune. February 19, 1995.

Fitts, Leroy. *A History of Black Baptists.* Nashville: Broadman Press, 1985.

Harlan, Louis R. and Raymond W. Smock, *The Booker T. Washington Papers. Vol. 12.* Urbana: University of Illinois Press, 1975.

Harvey, William J. ed. *"The 14th Preaching Team,"* Mission Herald. Vol 96, No. 2. Philadelphia: National Baptist Foreign Mission, March/April 1996.

Houston, Rev. M. H. *"Making Religion Work,"* Minutes of Rocky Mountain Association. Salt Lake City: Rocky Mountain Baptist Association, July 12-14, 1944.

Langon, Byrdie L. *Utah and The Early Black Settlers.* 1969.

Lucas, Reverend William A. *A New Deal In Religion.* Little Rock.

Lucas, Reverend William A. *"Moderator's Annual Address," Minutes of Rocky Mountain Association. Salt Lake City:* Rocky Mountain Baptist Association, July 12-14, 1944.

Lucas, Reverend William A. ed. *The Rocky Mountain Observer.* Salt Lake City: Calvary Baptist Church, 1945-1946.

Martin, Janet. *"History of Just-A-Portion,"* November 1996.

Monroe, Sarah, ed. *The Reflector.* Salt Lake City: Calvary Baptist Church, 1967.

Monroe, Reverend William I. *"Letter to Dwight S. Dobson."* Salt Lake City: Calvary Baptist Church, August 5, 1954.

New Hope Missionary Baptist Church of Salt Lake City, *Utah History and Aim,* 1968.

New Pilgrim Baptist Church, *"History."* Salt Lake City: New Pilgrim Baptist Church, 1973.

New Zion Baptist, Comp. *"A Condensed Biography of Our Pastor: Benjamin Jefferson Washington."* Ogden: New Zion Baptist. 1958.

Oliver, David H. *A Negro On Mormonism.* Salt Lake City: D. H. Oliver, 1963.

Polk's Salt Lake City Directory. Salt Lake City. 1890-1938.

Richmond, Charles E. *The Story of 60 Years.* Salt Lake City: Immanuel Baptist Church, 1946.

Savage, Sherman. *Blacks in the West.* Westport: Greenwood Press, 1979.

Smith, Elmer R. *"The Status of the Negro in Utah,"* Salt Lake City: University of Utah, 1956.

Souvenir Program 74th Annual Session, IGBA. August 6-10, 1991.

Spearman, Arnold. *"History of Utah Travelers."* Salt Lake City: Utah Travelers, 1996.

"Uplifting Tones of Utah Travelers To Be Heard," Eagle Newspapers. June 27, 1996.

True Vine Baptist Church. *"History."* Kaysville: True Vine Baptist Church. 1996.

Warrum, Noble. *Utah Since Statehood, Vol. 1.* Chicago: The S. J. Clarke Publishing Co., 1919.

Washington, Reverend B. J. *"Letter to the Members of the New Zion Baptist Church."* Ogden: New Zion Baptist Church.

Whaley, Monte. *"Park Will Replace Ogden Neighborhood."* Salt Lake City: *The Salt Lake Tribune.* June 10, 1996.

Williams, J. D. *"Mississippi, Utah, and Civil Rights,"* Pen Magazine. Salt Lake City: University of Utah. Autumn 1962.

Interviews

Anderson, George. Ogden, August 16, 1996.

Carter, Reverend Cal. Ogden, November 1, 1996.

DeBies, Ella Louise. Salt Lake City, February 1974.

DeBies, Frederick. Salt Lake City, July 31, 1996.

Finn, Clydies and Ray. Ogden, July 29, 1996.

Frye, Doris Steward. Salt Lake City, March 31, 1984 & November 10, 1996.

Miller, Edward. Salt Lake City, July 22 & 26 & August 5, 1996.

Morris, Anna Davison. Salt Lake City, May 2 & 15, 1996.

Morris, Taedra. Salt Lake City, May 23, 1996.

Nixon, Ernest. Salt Lake City, August 16, 1996.

Rucker, Mary West. Salt Lake City, August 16, 1996.

Smith, Mary Elizabeth Barker. Salt Lake City, February 22, 1983.

Styles, Nelson. Salt Lake City, September 9, 1996.

Tucker, Jesse & Thelma. Ogden, August 16, 1996.

Future Surveys

Council, Reverend Jerome. True Vine Baptist Church, Kaysville.

Davis, Reverend France A. Calvary Missionary Baptist Church, Salt Lake City.

Glass, Reverend George. New Pilgrim Baptist Church, Murray.

Lilly, Reverend Herbert J. New Life Baptist Church, Taylorsville.

Merritt, Reverend George. New Zion Baptist Church, Ogden.

Miller, Edward. Calvary Missionary Baptist Church, Salt Lake City.

Petty, Reverend Charles. Second Baptist Church, Ogden.

Simmons, Reverend Anthony. Unity Baptist Church, Salt Lake City.

Wilson, Reverend James. New Solid Rock Baptist Church, Salt Lake City.

Broad Ax. Salt Lake City & Chicago. 1895-1900.

Butte New Age. Montana. 1902-1903.

Deseret News. Salt Lake City, 1896-1996.

Salt Lake Herald. Salt Lake City. 1870-1902.

Salt Lake Tribune. Salt Lake City. 1880-1996.

Western Light. Salt Lake City. 1914.

Tri-City Oracle. Salt Lake City, 1902.

Utah Plain Dealer. Salt Lake City, 1897.

Biography of Reverend France A. Davis

The Reverend France A. Davis was born and reared on a Gough, Georgia farm, number eight of nine children to John H. and Julia Davis. After graduation from Waynesboro High and Industrial School, he attended Tuskegee Institute. He served four years during the Vietnam era in the USA Air Force as a jet mechanic. After honorable discharge, he earned degrees in Afro-American Studies from Merritt College, Arts and Humanities from Laney College, Rhetoric from University of California at Berkeley, Religion and Philosophy from Westminster College, Mass Communication from University of Utah, and Master of Ministry from Northwest Nazarene College.

Reverend France Davis and family

He moved to Utah in 1972 as a Communication Teaching Fellow and graduate student. After one year, he was appointed instructor and has continued to teach course in Communication and Ethnic Studies. He earned a Distinguished Teacher Award in 1974.

Presently, Reverend Davis serves as full-time Pastor of the Historic Calvary Missionary Baptist Church of Salt Lake City where he has been since February 1974.

He lectures widely on cultural and religious topics. He serves on community and national boards including OICs of America, Salt Lake County Career Service Council, Salt Lake City Housing Authority, and Salt Lake Convention and Visitors Bureau. He received an honorary Doctor of Humane Letters Degree from the U. of U., the Governor's Humanities Award, and the Utah State University Distinguished Service Award.

(9/9/96)

Index